DOUBLE YOUR PROFITS

DOUBLE YOUR PROFITS

78 Ways to Cut Costs, Increase Sales and Dramatically Improve Your Bottom Line in 6 Months or Less

BOB FIFER

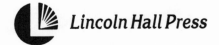 Lincoln Hall Press

Bob Fifer

DOUBLE YOUR PROFITS

Printed in the United States of America

Fourth Printing, December 1993

ISBN 0-9636888-0-4

To Mom and Dad,
Nancy,
Daniel, Rebecca, Lauren and Jonathan

TABLE OF CONTENTS

PART I

GETTING READY

STEP 1

WHO SHOULD READ THIS BOOK?

Anyone who cares about the profits of his or her business should read this book.

That, by the way, excludes a surprisingly large percentage of the managers in this country. Most mid-level managers, and many senior executives and even CEO's of *Fortune 500* companies are motivated by something other than profits: They want their businesses to grow, or harmonious employee relations and morale, or the ability to travel to interesting places and meet interesting people, or whatever else. Some owners of small businesses are more excited about the details of running an operation than they are about ensuring the financial health (i.e. the profitability) of their enterprise. To these audiences I say: Read the book if you'd like, and perhaps you'll better understand the importance of profitability and how to achieve it.

To those managers of large and small enterprises who truly *do* care about profits but are not fully pleased with their business' bottom-line results, I say: You *must* read this book. If you read it and take it seriously, you cannot avoid doubling, and probably tripling, the profitability of your business.

You can do so in either of two ways. Many of you will read the book, adopt those portions that are most relevant to your organization, and quickly see a dramatic rise in profits. Others will buy into the book's philosophy but decide that for a variety of reasons it's better to have an "outsider" implement the book's recommendations. The latter group should call me at the number included in the "About The Author" section at the back of the book. I run a company which specializes in coming into your business and doubling your profits. For our services we charge a very small fraction of the increased annual profits we will generate for you. (That's one of the few plugs for my company's services which you'll see in this book, but if I practice what I preach, I have to include at least a few.)

STEP 2

YOUR OWN COMMITMENT TO PROFITS

The perceptions and recommendations in this book are culled from two sets of experiences. During the last fifteen years, I have been a consultant to more than twenty percent of the *Fortune 500*, as well as numerous mid-sized and smaller companies throughout the Western world. I've seen every management tool, management style, fad, type of business, and strategy, and have the objective outside perspective to separate the good from the bad. Most striking has been the inappropriate focus on the fads and processes themselves, rather than on bottom-line results, but more about that later. During the last eleven of those fifteen years, I have also led my own company, Kaiser Associates, and have made it the most profitable company in its industry, by far. Having to meet a payroll and bring in the customers has been an experience that all of my consulting could never match. The combination of these two perspectives — the successful profit maximization of my own company and exposure to many less successful approaches in Corporate America and beyond — has driven me to write this book. If you do what I've done, you'll enjoy the same results that I have.

There is obviously a lot more to running a company than profits. You have to lead, motivate, and train employees, creatively define products and marketing strategies, ensure the efficient and high-quality "production" of your products or service, and so on. Kaiser Associates and I consult in all of these areas, and we can talk specifically about any of them if you would like. However, this book is focused on profits because that's where it all starts and ends. Profitable companies have the money to reward employees, build exciting career paths, and invest in new products, businesses and technologies. Less profitable companies inevitably sink into mediocrity in all ways — morale, product distinctiveness, and so on — because they wind up funding each part of the business half-heartedly and inadequately. Learn how to be very profitable and all else will follow. Try to do it all with mediocre or worse levels of profit, and you'll always be frustrated.

One important note: Doubling and even tripling profits is often conservative. Most of the businesses I've seen can have their profits multiplied by four, five, or even ten times if the steps outlined in this book are adhered to rigorously.

The specific steps to cut costs quickly are outlined in Part III of this book. The impact of these cost reductions will be a dramatic and permanent increase in your business' profits within two to six months. Steps to raise revenue and therefore further grow your bottom line are included in Part IV. Before I get to these topics, Part II describes the company culture — or more to the point, the *leader-*

ship style — necessary to implement the cost-cutting steps of Part III and the revenue-raising steps of Part IV. This leadership style is at the same time both easy and hard to adapt. It's easy in that it requires no advanced degree in business, accounting, technology, or any other endeavor, and no in-depth knowledge of any particular model or system. Most of the action steps required are common sense, pure and simple.

Then why do so few businesses practice them and achieve impressive levels of profitability? For one, because many managers don't truly care about profits, as discussed above. However, even many managers who *do* care about profits fail a second test: They lack the *absolute commitment to profits*, the *tough, determined resolve* to lead their organizations in a way consistent with the recommendations in this book. Doubling your profits (or more) requires a leader who is *focused, consistent, tough, and fair*, and who is willing to stretch himself or herself and others in the organization to be different and better than the status quo or the "average" manager of this world. That determined resolve, plus the step-by-step roadmap outlined in this book, are all that stands between you and doubled profits. To say it another way, if you *truly want* much greater profits, and you're willing to make the tough decisions, then doubled profits are easy to achieve.

So settle back and enjoy: It's a quick read, and the profits are waiting for you just around the corner!

PART II

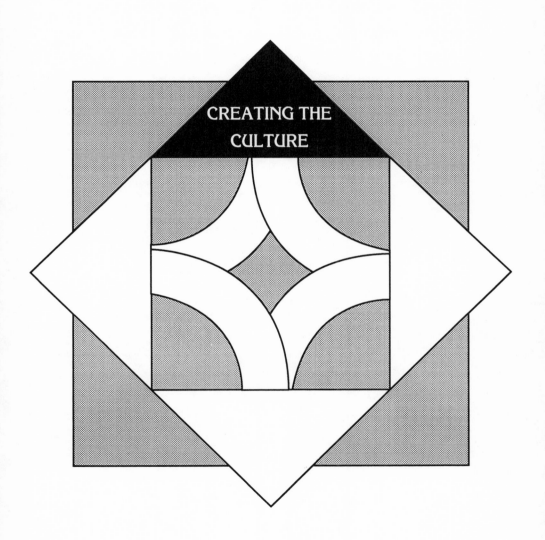

CREATING THE
CULTURE

STEP 3

SETTING THE STANDARD

Every organization needs a clear, single, over-riding goal. Some companies call this their "mission." The problem is that these goals or mission statements are off base nine times in ten.

About four in ten fail because the mission statement is nothing more than a pleasant-sounding collection of platitudes and buzzwords like, "We will satisfy our customers with superior products and service, by bringing out the best in our people, while being a responsible corporate citizen with regard to the environment and the communities in which we operate."

The other five of the ten contain more meaningful content, but fail because that content is not directed at the proper objective. These goals or mission statements assert that the primary purpose of the organization is to serve such-and-such markets, with the following products and services, and/or utilizing the following technologies. The problem is that markets, products, and technologies are all means to an end, not ends in themselves.

The end, the driving goal of any organization, should be one simple thing: to be the *best*. Nothing motivates employees, excites them about coming to work, *and* produces better bottom-line results, than to tell everyone in the organization that we as an organization and each of us as individuals will be the best, and will settle for nothing less.

STEP 4

WHAT DOES "THE BEST" MEAN?

The Best means three things:

1) We will never settle for the status quo. We will *always* drive as hard as humanly possible, in as many simultaneous directions as necessary, and as far as necessary, as long as we can identify things to achieve which we have not yet achieved.

This, by the way, does *not* mean "work long hours." My experiences have proven that there is little correlation between hours worked and results achieved, and I never drive my people to work long hours, or even measure or keep track of how many days or hours they're working. If you think about your day, week, or month, the *truly* worthwhile, *truly* value-creating things you've done are usually achieved during a few minutes or seconds when you have a crucial insight, make a crucial sale, or motivate a crucial subordinate, and those things are more likely to happen when you are working in a balanced, and not in a manic way. The same is true, at a different level, for most of your employees. The first critical ingredient to doubling your profits is creating a culture which says "The Best" means always thinking, always striving, always re-making yourself to be better, never being satisfied as long as there's something out there which we've not yet achieved.

2) Our organization will be a meritocracy. That means rewards — financial, career advancement, and psychic — will be allocated based on performance, not seniority,

"likeability," or anything else. Furthermore, rewards will be allocated *very* differentially: There will be a *very* wide spread in rewards among different people — as wide as the differences in performance that inevitably exist in any organization.

This is the first place where I'll lose some of my readers. Many managers are very uncomfortable with meritocracies. Most *Fortune 500* companies won't and don't do it. Meritocracies require managers to make tough decisions that affect people, and then tell those people to their faces. None of us wants to be a "mean" or "lousy" person, and sometimes we mistakenly feel that we are being "mean" to that half of the population which we reward less than the other half.

This sense of guilt is truly misguided. Like it or not — and most of us do when we consider the alternative — we live in a capitalist society. What each of us owes our employees is the *opportunity* to reach the top, and the training and support to help them get there. We do *not* owe them guarantees regardless of performance. Even more to the point, the manager who refuses to run a true meritocracy is being unfair to the better employees who are not being differentially rewarded for their superior performance.

If you are a relatively unsentimental, bottom-line-oriented manager, ask yourself, "Who would I rather have resentful: The better-performing employees, or the under-performers?" You'll always achieve better results by keeping the *top* half happy. (That, by the way, is the quickest way to determine, without seeing anyone's salary, whether an organization is a meritocracy. In a meritocracy, the bottom half complains. In a "seniority" or other system, the top-performing half complains.)

If you're a more soft-hearted manager, then do what I do. *Tell* your new employees *when you give them a job offer* that your organization is a meritocracy. If they perform well, the rewards will be great. If they don't, they won't be happy with the rewards, and they'll leave the company sooner or later, one way or another. Then after employees are hired (i.e. as you run your business day-to-day), communicate, in many ways all the time, that your company is a meritocracy. Define the terms of the meritocracy clearly: How will performance be measured, and what rewards will accrue to what levels of performance? Then deliver results — good and bad — that are consistent with the terms you defined. In other words, keep your promises. If you do it this way, you've been fair to all concerned, and you have nothing to feel guilty about. Even better, you'll find people of all sorts telling you over and over again that you're the best manager they've ever worked for.

Creating a true meritocracy means going beyond a "lip service" meritocracy that says people will be rewarded for performance, but which then creates only a relatively small (say ten or twenty percent) salary difference between the better and the poorer-performing people. It means promoting people when they're ready to contribute more and go the next step, regardless of age, years of service, or who else may be offended by being "leapfrogged" or passed over.

If you don't create a true meritocracy, people will never believe you're serious about performance, results, and profits. Your employees will think, "He says he wants profits, yet Bill is adding to the bottom line and not getting rewarded much more than Steve, who isn't." If you take dramatic and decisive actions obvious to all — promoting, paying, and firing people based on performance — you'll be amazed how fast people focus all their actions on improving the bottom line. Very few organizations have truly tried this, but it works every time. (Someone once said to me that the average time it takes an employee with a new results-oriented compensation system to focus his or her behaviors on achieving those results is approximately five to seven seconds.)

3) We're here to make a profit. In fact, we're here to make as much profit as we possibly can. Profit is the most accurate, most all-encompassing measure of whether we

truly are the best. Profits measure how much our customers value the products and services we deliver, and how efficiently we can organize and operate to deliver that value to our customers. Profits benefit all of us — profits provide cash for shareholders, for managers' and employees' compensation, and for investment which creates growth, which in turn creates rewarding career path opportunities. When the profits slow down, we all suffer.

STEP 5

NEVER APOLOGIZE FOR FOCUSING ON PROFITS

I have heard it said by academics or ineffective managers that "employees will never respond to profits as a driving motivation — what do they care if shareholders are enriched?" My real-world results disprove this statement completely. People not only respond to but *crave* clear, decisive measures of performance and results, both for their organizations and for themselves.

If you say "We're here to make shareholders rich," of course employees won't respond. If you say "We're here to be the *best* (*each* of us and *all of us together*); to creatively and vigorously strive to improve and achieve more in all ways possible; to reward each of us commensurate with our own performance; and to make it all possible by maximizing the bottom line," employees will understand, they'll be excited, and they'll be focused on the right target. The key is to communicate the overall message, and then to deliver the actions to show you mean it, as the rest of this book will describe.

Never apologize for maximizing profits: There's nothing to apologize for. If you're unapologetically excited about profits, your employees will be too.

STEP 6

RESULTS, NOT PROCESSES

I find mind-boggling the amount of time, energy, and money that companies, particularly large ones, spend on "processes." Some of these processes go under trendy, buzzwordy names: Total Quality, Team-Building, Strategic Planning, and so on. Each of these concepts has a value, a time, and a place. However, what has been lost at so many companies is any sense of proportion, any rigorous questioning of whether the effort expended is more than paying for itself in terms of bottom-line results.

Any excellent manager, anyone who wants to double profits, must have a built-in cynicism about "processes." *Any* investment in processes (and people's time is every bit as much of an investment as "out-of-pocket" expenditures) must be rigorously questioned: Assuming we buy the concept, do we really need a formal, extensive process to implement the concept, or can it be done in a quicker, more direct, more common sense way? If the answer is, "We need to get people to buy in," then ask, isn't there a quicker, more direct, more common sense way to communicate the importance of this concept to people than an extensive, inherently inefficient "process"? Never write a memo if telling someone will do, never call a meeting if a memo will do, never call a four-hour meeting if a one-hour meeting will do, never have two meetings if one will do, and *never* set up a process if two meetings will do. First of all, you'll directly save lots of time and money by eliminating wasted motion. Second of all, you'll convince people by the way you act that you're serious about focusing on results, not processes, and the savings will be multiplied many times over as they act in a similar fashion.

An over-focus on process is the refuge of weak or mediocre managers. I once saw the CEO of a nine-billion dollar, one-business company, who had been CEO for fifteen years, say, "We really don't have a company strategy. Let's set up a Task Force to come up with one, and have the Task Force report back to me in six months." If a manager who has run a business for fifteen years can't sit down and clearly state his or her strategy for the business in ten minutes or less, then what has that manager been doing all those years? (Answer: Probably setting up processes.) The reason the majority of companies over-invest in processes is:

1) The leader of the organization doesn't credibly communicate that results are the only thing we are here for.

2) It is easier for managers up and down the line to demonstrate that they have nice, shiny processes (i.e. that they are good at *spending* money), than to prove that they

are truly *making* money for the business, so they stick to the easier objective.

The average person left to his or her own devices will usually take the safe course of least resistance, and the average manager or employee is, on average, average. Unless as the leader of the organization you truly focus yourself and everyone else on the bottom line, on results, it won't happen. And a healthy, aggressive suspicion of all time-consuming, buzzwordy processes is one critical way to establish and communicate that focus.

STEP 7

STRATEGIC VS. NON-STRATEGIC COSTS

Let's get a little more specific. In my company, and in other superbly-run, very profitable companies I've seen (large and small), all costs are divided into two categories:

1) *Strategic costs* are defined as all those things that clearly "bring in business" and improve the bottom-line. Typical items in this category are the cost of salespeople (but not sales managers), advertising (*if* it's working), and *commercializable* R&D.

28

2) *Non-strategic* costs are all other costs, i.e. the costs necessary to run the business, but which don't clearly bring in more business. Administrative costs of all kinds fall in this category: managers, clerical support, rent or real estate cost, consultants, lawyers, accountants, computers, office supplies, and so forth. Often, this category also includes the costs of your manufacturing or service operations.

At my company, all cost reports (of which, by the way, there are very few — cost accounting can become just another "process" if you let it) are split into two categories: strategic and non-strategic costs. Whenever managers at my company have a meeting to discuss a new direction, a new investment, or how to enhance the bottom line, we automatically categorize each expenditure as strategic or non-strategic.

The reason is simple, and *very* powerful. My (or your) role as leader is to ensure that:

> ① We will *outspend* our competition for *strategic costs,* and spend this money in good times *as well as bad.*
>
> ② We will *ruthlessly cut non-strategic costs to the bone.*

This simple concept, applied with commitment and unwavering resolve, is more powerfully profit-maximizing than the most complex and detailed business treatise or process ever conceived. It is common sense, yet the very fact that ninety-five percent of the businesses and managers don't practice it creates an enormous competitive opportunity for those of us who do.

Outspending your competitors on strategic costs requires intelligence and judgment: You must distinguish those selling, marketing, and R&D expenditures that *truly* enhance the top and bottom lines from those which are wasteful and unlikely to pay off. There is no "formula" that anyone can give you to make that judgment: Excellent management is eighty percent art and only twenty percent science. Applying that intelligence and judgment on an ongoing basis — distinguishing the truly worthwhile strategic expenditures from non-strategic costs — is what makes your job challenging and fun. In the end, however, you must be able to identify enough *worthwhile* strategic expenditures to ensure that you are outspending your competition for strategic costs by a considerable margin, as a percentage of revenues if not in absolute dollars: By spending more on truly strategic costs, you build your business.

"Ruthlessly cutting non-strategic costs to the bone" requires an unwavering suspicion of every single non-strategic cost: Assume it can be eliminated unless proven otherwise. I truly believe that the average *Fortune 500* company has three managers for every one it needs (the average government agency has ten for one). The average *Fortune 500* company generates ten reports for every one it needs. (One manager I know implements the following system whenever he takes over a new business. He orders the *immediate* cancellation of all regular written or computer-generated reports. All the paper-generation and paper-moving is made to stop at once. Then people who are no longer receiving critical reports scream, and he reinstates those reports. At the end of two months, when all the screaming has stopped, only 40% of the original reports are ever requested and reinstated.) The average company has two square feet of office space for every one square foot it needs. It has *at least* three times the computer power it needs. (Have you ever calculated the capacity utilization of your investment in computers? Be prepared for a shock.)

Every fiber of me truly believes these things. Sometimes I go into a company and I discover that one or more of these beliefs is wrong at that company. *However, in order to profit-maximize, in order to cut non-strategic costs as much as possible, you must start with these beliefs and cynicism, and place the burden of proof on justifying costs, not on eliminating them.*

STEP 8

DON'T OVER-QUANTIFY THINGS

My parents are both mathematicians, and had my siblings and me learning calculus at the age of eight. In college I was a math major for two years, and watched the professors fill three blackboards proving a theorem that was intuitively obvious. That mathematical background has helped me in many ways, but in one crucial respect I as a businessman have had to forget everything I learned in math: Never spend a minute quantifying something you know the answer to already, and never spend more than a few minutes quantifying something when there's a reasonably high probability you know the right answer.

I recently spoke with the head of a small ($4.3 million) health care company that decided to pay a consultant $50,000 to quantify the size of the "total" market. This company knew its market share was well less than 1%, but wanted to know if the market was two or three or four billion dollars in size, i.e. whether its market share was two-tenths, one-and-a-half tenths, or one-tenth of one percent. Who cares??? The things this company does internally will have far more impact on its bottom line and on whether it achieves one-tenth of a percent more in market share than any quantification of this vast market. More to the point, that fifty thousand dollars could be spent in any number of ways that would directly lead to more sales (or, alternatively, not be spent but instead go *right* to the bottom line). This example may be extreme, but is not atypical. Most companies quantify all sorts of "nice-to-know" things; quantifying them costs time and money, but adds nothing to the bottom line.

I know another manager who insists that his people *forecast* future profits by the month, quarter, and year, and then update these forecasts frequently. He is tying up some of his best people generating these forecasts. As usual, there is also a detrimental second-order effort here: His people have picked up his subtle (or not-so-subtle) message that *accurately forecasting* profits is what he values and rewards.

No business ever made a penny on a forecast. *Optimizing* profits is what the business is here for, *not predicting* them. At most companies, I would eliminate 80% of the people resources dedicated to forecasting and number-crunching and spend that time on making money, not counting it.

At Harvard Business School I had a professor who taught us the following trick: Any time you are faced with a decision and can't make up your mind, do the following: Give yourself two seconds to decide. Not later, *right now.* Hurry, your two seconds are up. Okay you decided. Now go away and do all your homework and number-crunching and come back with your real decision. Ten times out of ten the "two-second" and the "heavily-researched" answer will turn out to be the same.

It's been many years since I learned that trick, and it's worked every time.

Most managers demand more data than they need. Superb managers are instinctual, making the right decision most of the time based on limited data. The quantification that less-skilled managers insist upon is in fact illusory: They wind up making decisions based upon that which can be quantified rather than that which is important. Most of the critical variables in any business decision can only be judged and guessed based on experience and instinct, not quantified. As the saying goes, better to be approximately right than exactly wrong.

DON'T OVER-DELEGATE,
AND DON'T UNDER-DELEGATE

It is unrealistic to expect large numbers of people in your organization to possess the *same* level of experience, judgment, and passion for profits that you have as the leader. Anything that is truly critical, that truly affects the bottom line, *you* must decide yourself. Everything else, all the work, all the necessary steps to set up the decision to be made or action to be taken, and all the time-consuming phone calls to be returned, you must delegate. Superb managers do 1% of the work but add more than 50% of the value to their organization, because they make the truly profit-enhancing decisions based on superior experience and judgment.

(That, by the way, is the reason why the recent brouhaha about executive compensation is a red herring. There is no doubt that Jack Welch at GE and other superb managers add far more value to their companies than their salaries. In fact, he probably adds more value *each week* than his annual salary by focusing his huge organization on profits. The mediocre CEO's and managers who never met a "process" they didn't love, who don't focus on profits and don't add true value, are overpaid. The issue is not executive compensation, but executive competence.)

Delegation is very much in fashion. In fact, it even has its own buzzword: "Empowerment." Empowerment is great if you are empowering people who have the skill and organizational means to focus on profits, or if they are empowered in other ways while you as a leader retain control over profits. Empowerment, however, is never an "absolute" good thing or an end in itself. Full empowerment of an organization which you have not focused on profits is an abdication of your most basic responsibility as a leader of the organization.

Weak managers "study" their businesses in detail (over-quantify) and manage their businesses only in general (over-delegate). Superb managers study their businesses only in general but manage in detail: The *important* details.

STEP 10

MAXIMIZING CUSTOMER SATISFACTION LEADS TO BANKRUPTCY

There are many ways to differentiate your company's products and to achieve superior customer satisfaction: By offering higher quality (e.g. Mercedes Benz), better service (Disney), a broader selection (Toys " Я " Us), a superior brand image (Federal Express), or some combination of the above. All of these are nice things to have, but all cost money to provide. The goal of the profit-maximizing organization is not to maximize differentiation, but to:

> Provide those elements of differentiation that the customer is willing to pay for, and not those that the customer is not willing to pay for.

This is not insensitive or selfish: This is survival and common sense. You are not doing customers a favor by building unwanted differentiation and costs into your products or services which raise the prices your customers have to pay. Sooner or later, they'll switch to a supplier smart enough to include the right but exclude the wrong types of differentiation.

The Honda Accord, with only four colors and two options packages, vanquished competing General Motors car lines which had almost infinite varieties of colors, radios, engines, seat cushions, and pin-stripe designs, all of which added to GM's manufacturing/logistics complexity and costs. Honda eliminated the costs of this unneeded variety, put some of the savings in its pocket as superior profits and gave the rest of the savings back to the customer in the form of superior, *standard-package* quality.

L'eggs revolutionized the pantyhose industry and created huge profits by understanding that women didn't need to pay high department-store margins to get glitzy department-store ambiance when they made a routine, un-glamorous purchase of an every-day item.

Striking the right balance as to what to sell your customer is where the profits are, where the greatest judgment is required, and where the true fun of running a business lies. You *must* conceive a way to offer superior differentiation, or you have nothing to sell. However, the vast majority of people in your organization — the salespeople, the engineers, the marketers, the entrepreneurs — are trained to *add* differentiation. Who's trained to *eliminate* those costly elements of differentiation that the customer is not (or no longer) willing to pay for? The answer is precious few, and that's why it's so critical for you to train the organization to create a culture of "What is the customer willing to pay for?"

"Maximizing Customer Satisfaction" is a platitude, and a cop-out. (If you truly want to maximize the customer's satisfaction, cut your price to zero or give him or her a free trip to Hawaii and a free car once a month. You'll also maximize your own bankruptcy.) Forcing yourself to separate out the differentiation the customer is willing to pay for from "it's-nice-to-have-but-I-won't-pay-for-it" is what is best for your customer, you, and your bottom line.

STEP 11

STRATEGIC VS. NON-STRATEGIC TIME

Just as there is strategic and non-strategic cost, there is strategic and non-strategic time:

- *Strategic time* is defined as anything you do that *produces profits.*

- *Non-strategic* time is defined as that which is "busy" and succumbs to the requirements of "processes," but which does not contribute to profits.

Your role as a superlative leader is to communicate by your every action and every utterance that

44

the former is appreciated and the latter is frowned upon. If you change the way you manage your own time and encourage those around you to do the same, you'll see a myriad of changed behaviors by the people up and down the organization who look to leadership for signals as to what to do.

People respond to a host of your non-verbal signals. How do you act, how focused are you on results, how much of a hurry are you in, how intolerant are you of wasteful, time-consuming parts of the day? Think about the last meeting which you led. Did nine people *really* need to be in the room for four hours? Did they *all* benefit from — or rather, contribute anything to — each presentation? Was it crucial for Janet to sit through the whole meeting? Michael? Karen? What you are inadvertently communicating is that process and protocol are more important than results. Couldn't Karen have spoken on the phone to a few customers (or better yet, potential customers) during the time she spent listening to Michael's presentation? Which would have been a more profitable use of her time?

Literally a hundred times a day you spend time on something wasteful or allow wasteful time to be spent in your organization. I'm not suggesting that you eliminate the office basketball pool, time spent at the water cooler, or the occasional taking off for a round of golf: those are *fun.* What I *am* saying you must eliminate is the myriad of time-wasting meetings, forms to be filled out, and other activities that are *neither* fun *nor* profit-producing: They are there merely because of force of habit and lack of management rigor and leadership.

The message a superb leader communicates to his or her organization is:

A) We are a *great* company, an incredibly exciting place to be;

B) We are here to make a *profit;*

C) We have *so much more* yet to accomplish, *so much* uncaptured opportunity;

D) Every ounce, every fiber, every dollar, every minute of our organization will focus on realizing our potential and making a profit. We will ruthlessly pursue anything that contributes to that end;

E) Every other (i.e., non-strategic) dollar, every other minute will be ruthlessly stamped out. What is it you (employees) want anyway? To work for a great company or to merely punch a timeclock? When you bring in a new customer or eliminate an unnecessary cost you are helping make a great company. When you sit in a meeting or fill out a form or crunch numbers or fiddle with technology no one will buy you are helping sink the company and yourself into mediocrity.

It all ties together. The inevitable tough decisions become palatable, even *attractive* to employees if you show with your actions that you as a leader are focused on results and on building a great future. However, the overall message will be credible *only if* it is reflected in your actions as you manage the business day-to-day and hour-to-hour.

STEP 12

A SENSE OF URGENCY

There are virtually no important management tasks that take six months to complete. Yet how many Task Forces, consultants, or committees are given that long or longer to do their job (or worse, to come up with "a plan," but to actually *do* nothing)? How many heads of small businesses *know* the things that need to be done that are truly important to the future of their businesses, but take many months or years to get to them because they're "just too busy?"

The first thing I do the morning of every work-day is divide everything I have to do that day into three lists. The first list includes anything that brings in new business (i.e. raises revenue) or eliminates costs. (These are the *only* two ways you can create profit, since profit equals revenue minus cost.) The second list includes things I have to do to "maintain" existing business or keep an existing internal operating system running. The third list includes all the things that someone expects or wants me to do, but which really add no value to the bottom line. I *never* start on my second list until I've done everything on my first list, and *never* start on my third list until I've done everything on my second list. I *always* get everything on my first list done before noon that day, when my mind is most alert and my mood most constructive. I always get everything on my second list done by mid-afternoon. Sometimes I finish my third list, and sometimes I decide I've had enough, and I go home.

This sequence, by the way, is the *opposite* of the normal human tendency. The most important tasks (i.e. list 1) are usually the hardest to conceptualize and implement, so the tendency is to procrastinate and do the less threatening, less critical tasks (list 3) first: Hence the businessperson who is always "too busy" to do the most important things.

You have to make sure that the most important things are completed with the most urgency, but there's more to creating a sense of urgency. You must insist on a culture that says nothing important takes more than a few minutes or a day or a week, or a month if it's truly complex, to complete. *Always* set deadlines in the very near term: If you stick to this, people always will meet the deadlines, not by working all night but by eliminating non-value-producing tasks from their schedules. That is the *real* benefit of tight deadlines. My philosophy is to *always keep resources very scarce*, because that is the *only* way to force people to soul-search about which tasks are truly value-producing and which are not. The opposite is also true: Give people more time, and as the very true cliché goes, time spent on a task will always expand to the time allowed.

Never call a meeting to discuss: *only* call a meeting to decide. Never, or *rarely*, accept "let me think about it and call you back" as an answer: What more are they going to know later to make the decision that they don't already know now? Make the decision *now*, so that "later" they can make *another* decision or achieve something else and therefore be twice as productive.

A stubborn impatience to do things *now* is a powerful producer of profit. It also engenders an enormous respect from those in your organization. No one respects procrastinators, and everyone admires "doers." Every time I'm in one of our offices I ask people to do more things: You'd think they'd dread seeing me. The truth is quite the contrary. Person after person has told me that when I'm away from the office things are uninspiring, but when I come in my *sense of urgency* and the way that I project it is contagious and exhilarating and makes them truly charged up about their own jobs.

Create and maintain a strong sense of urgency in your business, and it will pay you back a thousand times over in the increased focus and productivity of everyone in the organization.

STEP 13

TRANSLATING THE CULTURE INTO ACTION

There is a never-ending feedback loop of culture, actions, and results. You help create a profit-focused culture with words, but you make it credible by your actions. The actions produce results, which in turn allow you to reward the people who deserve to be rewarded. Those rewards make people believe in the culture, and as a result the culture is strengthened. All of your people start to act in a profit-focused way — The results are multiplied, and the loop starts all over again.

It's time now to turn to some of the more specific, nitty-gritty actions you should take to double your profits. I'll start first with Cutting Costs — the topic of Part III.

PART III

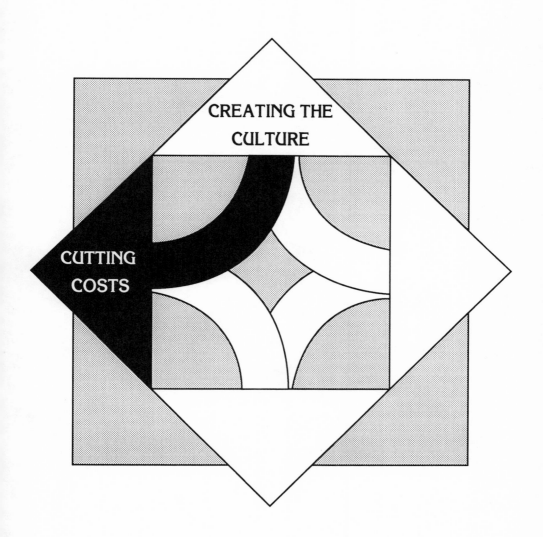

CREATING THE
CULTURE

CUTTING
COSTS

STEP 14

EVERY COST IS UP FOR GRABS

The first step towards reducing costs is to see *every* cost as, at best, a necessary evil.

So many people in our society see costs as a *plus*. More costs mean a bigger organization to run, a larger bureaucracy to be administered, more respect from your friends and neighbors. (I'm always struck by *how* people inquire about the size of my business: They ask me how many employees I have, not the number of satisfied clients or the amount of revenue. The answer is that we are a relatively small firm in terms of employees (costs), but a large firm in terms of revenue. Of course, it's the revenue, or rather the difference between revenue and cost, that is the true measure of success.)

I truly see all costs as at best necessary evils. In fact, I say to my business associates, "I don't believe in costs," because I don't: Costs are something to be driven mercilessly out of any business to the maximum extent possible.

The day-to-day manifestation of this policy is that I (and you) need to see *every* cost as "up for grabs," i.e. as something that you should try to find a way to eliminate. When I visit a company and see unused office space or a receptionist reading a magazine or an idle computer or a paper-shuffling, non-value-adding manager, I instantly and instinctively see the opportunity to increase profits. No cost should be "absolutely" sacred: No manager, system, perk, or capital expenditure. Sure, many costs will withstand your or my scrutiny and prove to be justified; but your mindset *going in* has to be to try to eliminate every cost that you encounter.

What I'm really talking about is a "zero-based" budgeting of the mind (but not the formal process).

Don't assume anything *has* to be done the way it is. Instead, always ask the question, "If I eliminated this cost, would I *really* lose revenue or profits? How and where?" If you can't figure out how and where, then you don't need the cost.

All of this (and what follows) applies *particularly* well to "Non-Strategic Costs" (see Step 7), but also to Strategic Costs. Strategic Costs (e.g. salespeople or advertising) are profit-producing in *principle*, but only if spent well. You must eliminate all non-profit-producing strategic costs so as to leave more money for truly productive expenditures.

STEP 15

CUT COSTS FIRST, ASK QUESTIONS LATER

The common mistake that managers (and the President and the Congress of the United States) make is to be too cautious in cutting cost: "Let's not cut Cost A unless we're *sure* it's the right decision."

Well, that's backwards. It should be "Let's not *keep spending* Cost A unless we're sure we need that cost." I once told a CEO whom I assisted for five years that we must put the burden of proof in his organization on *spending* money, not on cutting expenditures. He said if that was all I accomplished, I could do no greater service for his organization.

The comforting thing about cutting costs is that, if you *do* make a mistake, somebody will always tell you and you can add the cost back. All the pressures in the typical organization are to *add* costs. Hire three new people instead of six in Department X, and they'll inevitably come back and tell you how overworked they are. Buy 10 PC's instead of 15, and the requisition request for 5 more will inevitably come. Cut costs too much, and you'll get lots of chances to correct your mistake. *Spend* too much, and that money is gone forever. You *must* change the mindset of your organization, starting with your own. If in doubt, *cut more* and *spend less*. The cost-spending tide is so great that only a very resolute and strong force in the opposite direction will successfully stop it.

STEP 16

SET "ARBITRARY," NON-NEGOTIABLE BUDGETS

One management technique to "cut costs first and ask questions later" is to judgmentally set very tough budgets, and leave it up to the leader of that function or business unit to figure out how to stay within the budget.

One professional services firm I work with has revenue of $50 million per year, and was used to spending $250,000 per month on office supplies and services. After a cursory review, it became clear that in the past no one had seriously attempted to control or minimize these costs. I told them that, in my experience, office supply costs are 40% lower in profit-focused firms than in the "typical" (i.e. their) company.

We set a budget, somewhat arbitrarily (i.e. *judgmentally*, not based on some expensive quantitative study), equal to 60% of (i.e. 40% less than) previous expenditures. The head of the business declared that *that's all the money there is, that is all the checks we will write*, so *don't* exceed the budget. We did nothing else.

The budget was met the first month, and has since been met for twenty-two months in a row. Savings have equalled $1.2 million per year, or 2.4 "margin points" (i.e. 2.4% of sales). The time spent to achieve these savings was the fifteen minutes it took us to make the decision, another five to write the memo announcing the budget, and thirty to brief and motivate the relevant supervisors.

We went back later to look at how the savings were achieved. As it turns out, each supervisor was creative and forceful in eliminating redundancies, waste and unnecessary "creature comforts" (Does *everyone* need the fanciest, wood-panelled whiteboards in his or her office?). What made the cost cut work was the sequence in which it was done. We didn't ask each supervisor to see what cost cuts could be achieved and report back to us, and then use that input to set a budget. In my experience, that approach would have yielded savings of *at most* five percent. Instead, we set a budget based on our experience and judgment, and let the supervisors react. If we cut too low (in this case, we didn't), we would have heard about it, and ultimately would have added back to the budget.

There are *many* cost areas in your organization — some big, some small — that would benefit from this approach. The added profits are sitting there waiting for you to capture them. All you need is the decisiveness and experience to make it happen.

STEP 17

MAKE THEM COME ASK THE BOSS

Here's another *highly* effective means to achieve sure-fire cost reduction.

For the targeted cost item, don't eliminate it, and don't even set a budget. Merely announce that anyone wanting to spend money in that area has to contact you first and ask you personally for your permission.

I have done this for many discretionary items, such as new furniture, new staff employees, and the hiring of certain types of outside services (e.g. "temps," market research, etc.). The results have been *superb*. Some employees write me concise, convincing arguments for why they need the money, and I approve those requests. These requests are fairly rare; the rest of the previously-spent money is never requested, and no longer spent.

Everyone loves to spend money in anonymity. *No one* wants to be singled out and to have to go to the boss to ask for money, *unless* his or her cause is a worthy one. This *simple* technique separates almost perfectly the worthwhile expenditures from the wasteful ones.

Make sure that you make the process by which they make their cost request of you an onerous one. Do *NOT* create a simple form for them to fill out. Be *somewhat* of an intimidating person to approach. Always scrutinize requests critically, and disallow as many as possible. With that reputation, the system will work: Most will be discouraged, but the good expenditures will still get through. If you're too approachable and too much of a "softee," the system won't do you as much good.

The bottom line of Steps 16 and 17 combined is: *Never* spend money by accident or routine. Always make the spending of money a difficult process that must jump through several hoops to prove its worthiness.

STEP 18

NO COST IS TOO SMALL TO WORRY ABOUT

This principle is very simple. Show your employees you care about saving money on a $10 item, and *boy* will they look for savings on larger items. *There are no exceptions* to the "necessary evil" of costs. Give in a foot, and you'll slip a mile. Scrutinize *every* cost, and your message will be taken seriously. Furthermore, there is a *surprising* amount of money to be made in cutting so-called "minor" costs, since those are precisely the costs that no one has ever bothered to look at before!

Be consistent. *Every* cost must prove its worthiness.

STEP 19

DON'T WORRY — THEY'LL RESPECT YOU

Some managers are afraid to take an aggressive approach to cost-cutting because they'll be considered "vicious" or "petty" or "anti-people." If you're good at what you do, this fear is unfounded.

Toughness plus competence engenders respect of you, not resentment. Toughness plus incompetence or mediocrity will engender resentment. So if you're good enough, your toughness will not be resented.

The irony is, most managers *are* good enough, and don't realize it. As I've said before, a focus on cost-cutting and profits and on being the best is mostly determined resolve, and not rocket science. It is relatively easy to be a good, profit-maximizing manager, *if* you're determined to do it. It's merely a question of adopting the right mindset and taking the plunge. If you're resolute, you'll be good, and if you're good, they'll respect you more than resent you. That respect will make you even tougher and better, and you'll be in a very productive "positive feedback loop," as the psychologists say.

STEP 20

EMPLOYEES ARE MUCH MORE ADAPTABLE THAN YOU REALIZE

Every time I eliminate a cost someone says to me, "You can't possibly expect such-and-such an employee or employee group to live with that." Six months after the change is implemented, no one can remember the way it was before. Employees adapt quickly to each new level of expectation.

Five years ago I moved my company's Washington, D.C. office from a downtown to a suburban location, saving hundreds of thousands of dollars in rent in the process. Some of the managers in the firm argued that it couldn't be done, because we recruit some people straight from college, and they wouldn't want to live in suburbia or commute from the city (where the night-life is). They made this argument repeatedly and strenuously.

My answer was, we're a great firm with great jobs. Employees will adjust, and any long-term loyal employee who has been unduly inconvenienced could even be compensated for his or her trouble. However, to avoid saving the cost made no sense.

Last year, we ended the use of messenger services for all packages delivered in the same metropolitan area. The savings were twenty thousand dollars per year, not a trivial amount for a firm our size. When I announced the change, people said, "How can you do this? How will the packages get there?"

Well, six months later, we've adjusted. Some packages get mailed. Employees drive some over themselves on the way home from work. Some of our suppliers now drive things over rather than charge us forty dollars for a messenger. The point is, what seemed impossible is now routinely integrated into our firm's day-to-day life.

This is almost always the case. Because you're so used to your company's routines, some cost-cutting changes seem drastic. However, with the passage of a short period of time, these so-called "drastic" changes become routine and quite harmless. Employees adjust their expectations and routines. Money is freed up for more important expenditures, including employees' salaries.

STEP 21

START WITH THE MOST PAINLESS PLACE —
SUPPLIERS

Many managers feel the imperative to cut costs, but are reluctant to impose "pain" on their organization. The most painless way to reduce costs is to aggressively manage the prices paid to suppliers for goods and services.

Suppliers also represent a *large* source of potential cost savings: Significant savings can be realized with relatively little effort. What percent of your business' total cost is comprised of purchased goods and services? For many businesses the number is as high as 50% or even 70%, and rarely is it lower than 20%. If purchased goods and services (or "procurement" or "purchasing" for short) equals 50% of your total cost, and you realize savings of only 8%, you've added roughly four "margin points" to your bottom line, which will have a *big* percentage impact on profits.

One of the reasons that purchasing represents such a significant profit opportunity is that it is largely ignored by the managers who run businesses. Managers get excited about customers, and manage that end of the business aggressively, and are also very aware of employees, and manage them purposefully as well. However, purchasing is often thought of as an "administrative" problem, a "detail" not worthy of senior management's attention, or "Joe's problem — he's my purchasing guy and I let him worry about it."

I often ask managers the following question: "If you were offered a million dollar bonus if you could raise your margin by two points by the end of this year, and no bonus if you do not, where are you most sure to get the two points — by making customers pay more or by getting suppliers to charge less?" They *always* answer "suppliers." That is a tacit admission that they are not doing as good a job managing the prices they pay suppliers as they are other areas of their business.

I was once retained to lower the costs of a company which manufactures railroad box cars. On the first day that I arrived, they sent me on a plant tour and had me meet with all the key manufacturing executives. "Cut costs in the plant," the head of the business told me.

After a while, I stopped the schedule and asked to meet with the head of the business for a few minutes. "What percent of your cost is manufacturing, and what percent is purchasing?" I asked. After some paper shuffling, he replied that they purchase the sides, ends, and undercarriage of the box car, equal to 80% of total cost. Manufacturing represented 10% of cost, and other "white collar" costs totalled 10%. "When was the last time you studied how to reduce manufacturing cost?" I asked. "Oh, we do it every two years," he assured me, "But it obviously is not enough. We still are high cost relative to competition and we're still not making a good profit." I next asked, "When's the last time you studied how to reduce purchasing cost?" He answered, "Well, we just buy steel and paint and so forth. Harry does a pretty good job of it." Well, I explained that a 5% reduction in purchasing cost would lower total cost 4% (5% of 80%). In order to realize similar savings, manufacturing cost would have to be lowered *forty* percent (40% X 10% = 4%), an impossibility.

We attacked purchasing cost, and actually realized 9% savings, or 7.2% (9% of 80%) of total cost. This move *alone* doubled the company's profits.

STEP 22

NEVER LET YOUR PURCHASING PERSON NEGOTIATE PRICE

The worst person in the world to negotiate price with your suppliers is your purchasing person. He or she talks to that supplier all the time, knows the supplier well, and can't help but develop some sort of personal bond with the supplier. He or she cannot then be expected to be absolutely as tough as nails and negotiate the best possible price, now and repeatedly in the future. What's needed is some exogenous shock to the relationship that forces the supplier to aggressively lower its price.

I don't mean that the purchasing person *literally*

cannot negotiate with the supplier. I mean that you should not leave the negotiation to the purchasing person *alone*, but instead need a way to force the purchaser to squeeze the supplier as much as possible.

Here are a few ways to introduce this necessary "exogenous" shock.

STEP 23

YOU NEED A "BAD GUY"

Someone has to be the heavy. It can be "corporate," or the head of the business. It can be a specially-appointed cut-purchasing-costs "czar" as one company I work closely with has done very effectively. It can be a clerical or administrative person with particularly good negotiating skills and a can-do, bottom-line attitude. (When you find one of these people, hold onto them for dear life, and for *all* life. They pay for themselves a hundred times over.) Or, it can be an outside consultant as long as you give the consultant the authority to go out and actually implement, and not just recommend.

Whoever it is, you *must* have a bad guy. The role of the bad guy is to scrutinize the cost of each purchased item (starting with the biggest amounts of money first) and issue tough, so-called "arbitrary" price constraints which the purchasing person then "reluctantly" relays to the supplier. "I can't help it, George, but Laura says this is the top price I can pay. I don't think it's fair, but I can't help it any more than you can. Do you want our business (at this new price) or don't you?"

The first rule of any negotiating course or textbook is to tie *your* negotiator's hands: Empower the negotiator to accept concessions, but not to give them. Apply this rule to your purchasing function.

STEP 24

DECLARE FREEZES AND CUTS

Here's a way to increase your profits almost immediately. Send a letter to *all* of your suppliers stating that times are tough and henceforth (or for twelve or eighteen months) you will accept *no* price increases, so don't even bother sending them along.

Half your suppliers will ignore your letter (although if you stick to it, half of that half will eventually cave in). The other half will freeze their prices, and cancel any scheduled price increases. You've just saved your business a lot of money, this year.

And now for the advanced course. Send the same letter, but instead of declaring a freeze declare an across-the-board 3% reduction. Make sure the letter is from someone "high up" and intimidating — preferably the CEO. Tie your negotiator's (purchasing agent's) hands. You'll be amazed how many of your suppliers roll back prices 3%. For those who don't, when the bill comes have your purchasing agent deduct the 3% from the bill and say, "Didn't you read my CEO's letter? What are you trying to do, get me fired?" Another large group of suppliers will give in at this point.

STEP 25

GO TO BID, FREQUENTLY

Try this test on your business. For the largest (i.e. most dollars) fifty items you buy, when was the last time you put each out to competitive bid? Chances are that you have many items that have not been put out to serious competitive bid in more than twelve months. For some, it will be three years, five years, or never.

Every price increase you accept for any item without a competitive bid is wasted money. (Try announcing to your suppliers that every price *increase* triggers an automatic, *serious* competitive bid. You will instantly start receiving only half as many price increases.)

For every important or even semi-important item, do one of two things a *minimum* of once a year: Either conduct a truly competitive, aggressive price bid, or, if that's too much trouble, just tell your suppliers that you're doing it. It works almost as well.

We have one supplier of office services on which we spend a lot of money. We've been using her company for six years. Last month, I sent someone to ask her to lower her price to us, and she said "Sorry, but it's already pretty low. I can't lower it any more." I sent my person back to remind her that we represent 10% of her total business and *surely* she can do better. She responded, "I really appreciate your business, but I already give you the best price of all my customers. I can't go any lower." Finally, I had my person call her to tell her that we were terminating the relationship, and bidding it to four other suppliers. She was welcome to bid it if she wanted, but since we already knew that her price was unacceptable to us, she probably shouldn't bother. She lowered her price *that day, 20%,* and told us she was going to study the situation further to find other ways to cut the price.

We never did go to bid, nor did we intend to. It wasn't necessary, as I knew she couldn't afford to lose our business.

STEP 26

WHEN SUPPLIERS SAY "NO,"
HIT THEM AGAIN AND AGAIN

The previous example points out another lesson: "No" from a supplier rarely means "no way," it just means "I'd rather not."

I'm struck by how many people accept the first answer as *the* answer. It's just a negotiation! Ask again, and again, and again, and they'll usually give in, if only because they're getting tired of talking to you and want to get on with other work they have to do.

Remember that the person at the supplier that you are negotiating with is a salesperson, and salespeople are usually the world's worst negotiators.

They want to *make the sale*, and care less about price. Make them *truly* believe that the sale depends upon lowering the price, and the price will come tumbling down.

STEP 27

BUDGET 15% SAVINGS FOR PURCHASED PRODUCTS, AND 30% FOR PURCHASED SERVICES

For *services*, 30% savings is achievable. Your suppliers' fixed costs are often high, and any incremental business at almost any price contributes to profits. For many *products*, 15% savings (or higher) are achievable, if only because you've neglected being price-aggressive for so long, and have cumulatively accepted a lot of unnecessary price increases.

Will 30%, and 15%, be achievable for every item? Of course not. However, *higher* savings are achievable for some items. Thirty percent and fifteen percent are good, *aggressive* savings "budgets" on average across your purchased services or products. If you "fail" and achieve only 75% of the budgeted savings, you've still made a heck of a lot of money.

STEP 28

FIND OUT WHAT YOUR COMPETITORS PAY

After you think you've wrung all the savings out of your suppliers that can possibly be achieved, there's one more step that will drive the price of some of your key purchased items a lot lower. Find out whom your competitors buy from, and what they pay. Inevitably, one or more of your competitors is paying significantly less, even for so-called "commodity" items such as commodity chemicals, corrugated containers (boxes), or paper. Then, *use* that data. You can go to your competitor's supplier, and ask for the same deal. Alternatively — and this will work most times — you can share the data with your own supplier. Chagrined, because he had been telling you all along that you were getting the best price, he will usually match the lower price immediately.

How do you find out what your competitors are paying their suppliers? Sometimes you can find out from the "grapevine" or from sources you've cultivated in the past. If not, my company has a group which specializes in finding out competitors' supply costs for our clients. It's easy and it's inexpensive. However you do it, find out what your competitors pay for your big ticket purchased items. The effort will pay for itself a hundred times over, every time.

STEP 29

CUT YOUR USE OF PURCHASED GOODS AND SERVICES

As much opportunity as there is to cut the price you pay for purchased items, there are potentially even greater savings to be derived from cutting your use of purchased goods and services.

Examples range from the mundane but financially significant, to the essential and financially *very* significant. Does anyone *aggressively* control your use of office supplies? How about your purchases of computer hardware, software, and services? (More about these later.) How aggressively do you manage waste in your plant? How about your use of outside "consultants": engineering consultants, personnel consultants, management consultants, and so forth? Does everyone at your company routinely, and without any controls, use express delivery services, whether they truly need them or not? (One large financial services company located in a New York City skyscraper discovered it was spending thousands of dollars per month on Federal Express packages delivered to co-workers *in the same building* as the sender. When queried, one sender said he had to use Fed Ex to send something from the forty-second to the thirteenth floor because it was quicker and more reliable than the internal company mail system. To which my reply was, let me introduce you to the elevator.)

At every company, the *use* of many (if not all) categories of purchased goods and services is viewed as a God-given right, a convenience which it would be "rude" to question. Well, even a very rough approximation of the potential savings reveals the following greater truth: Failure to intelligently and aggressively minimize usage of purchased items represents not only a large amount of squandered profits, but also an abdication of leadership in an area critical to the company.

In the steps that follow, I'll discuss a number (but certainly not all) of the purchased categories where usage can be cut.

STEP 30

COMPUTERS

Computers are probably the single most misman-
aged item in business today. Many managers were
educated before the widespread use of personal computers became common, and are at a disadvantage
relative to their younger, computer-literate subordi-
nates. Even computer-literate managers and workers possess to varying degrees a fear of the more
intricate elements of computer technology. Even
more damaging, many in our society and our businesses are dazzled by the capabilities of a Macintosh
or mainframe, and view ever-advancing computer
sophistication as a must-have end in itself, whether

or not the advancement *truly* pays for itself in cost savings.

The combination of ignorance and the "sex appeal" of computers leads many managers to abdicate responsibility and leave computer purchasing decisions in the hands of the "MIS" manager and individual users. Well, that's like letting your interior decorator decide on his or her own how much to spend furnishing your home.

Recently, someone in my company asked me to authorize a series of hardware and software upgrades to the area of our firm which produces the published reports we deliver to our clients. "Why do we need to spend the money?" I asked. "Because our system is outdated," was the reply. "Having the most advanced computer system is not an objective of our company," I said, "Making money is. Tell me again, why do we need these upgrades?" He answered, "Because of our outdated system, our people sometimes have to wait three or four minutes to load an old file to start working on it again. Think of the money we'd save!" "Fine," I said, "Let's think of the money. What do we pay the average person in this department? How often each week do they have to wait three or four minutes? What is the cost in terms of salary (assuming there is nothing for them to do while they wait, an unlikely assumption in itself)? What is the cost of the upgrade that would "solve" the problem? Over what period of time will the savings in terms of time pay for the upfront cost of the upgrade?"

We did the math. After twenty-six years, we would break even. Needless to say, we did not purchase the upgrade.

I am amazed at how often people argue that "productivity gains" are the reason to spend more money on their computer system, yet how rarely anyone actually *quantifies* those gains and does the break-even analysis on the upfront cost. You wouldn't (I hope) build a manufacturing plant that way, yet you buy computers that way!

Obviously, many, many computer purchases are justified. But many more aren't. A good, profit-maximizing manager must take responsibility for determining which is which.

Another huge area of cost savings is the capacity utilization of your computer systems, particularly your PC's. At all big (and many small) companies I go to now, *everyone* has a PC on his or her desk. Some employees use these computers frequently, and need them. Others use them fifteen minutes a day, or every third day. That's a lot of money sitting there unused! Get rid of it, and in many cases it won't be missed. In other cases, a shared computer in a common area will work just fine.

Do you want to increase your profits, now? Put an immediate freeze on all PC purchases. If someone new needs one, take one from someone who's barely using it. It will take you years to catch up with all the unused capacity. (You'll actually *never* catch up with it. Your people will argue they need new PC's because the old ones are obsolete before you ever catch up with unused PC capacity.)

A final note on computers: The sex appeal/fun factor causes many of your employees to do things on a computer that are less expensive to do by hand.

I have seen hundreds of computer-generated reports, spreadsheets, and the like that take longer to set up and input the data than the average person would have taken to do the same without a computer. A neighbor of mine (a business executive) recently invested in a pay-bills-by-phone system from the local telephone company. It is physically impossible to pay a bill by phone faster than you can write a check and put it in an envelope! The phone system wastes time and money, but it's fun.

That's fine if he's at home, but not when similar behavior is hurting your business.

Master the management of computers. However, do *not* fall in love with computers, *or* run from them. It will cost you a ton of money if you do.

STEP 31

R&D

An older, and in some cases much bigger problem is R&D.

Executives avoid scrutinizing R&D for a similar reason that they avoid managing computers. Executives are used to being the most knowledgeable and "best" person in the room. When they talk to scientists and engineers about R&D, they feel dumb. The solution most pick is to leave R&D to the scientists, to "trust" that they know what they are doing.

The good news is that the scientists *do* know science. The bad news is that they *don't* know management or how to make a profit. Unfortunately, when you leave R&D to them you're trusting them to do both.

People used to say that Bell Labs was the best R&D organization in the world. "What does that mean?" I would ask. "Well, they have more Ph.D.'s doing more advanced work in more leading-edge areas than any other R&D organization in the world." Probably true. Unfortunately, it also may have been true that *for the money* they brought fewer new commercializable products to market in a timely fashion than any R&D organization in the world. Were they the best, or the *worst*, R&D organization?

As with much in this book, there is no magic to saving money in R&D. It simply requires your rigorous attention. Some of the rules are:

- Scrutinize each category of expenditures within R&D as closely as you do for other parts of the company with which you are more naturally comfortable.

- Do *NOT* let the scientists or engineers talk science with you. If they can't explain IN

ENGLISH the value of a particular project to the company, don't fund it. *Insist* on this, and do not let your frustration with your lack of scientific expertise cause you to give up and give in. If they can't explain the value of their potential breakthrough in layman's terms, how are you ever going to manage it and how are your salespeople ever going to sell it?

- Ask your R&D (or engineering or other technical department) people to divide all of their projects and expenses into five categories:

1) Pure, basic R&D;

2) New product R&D;

3) Improvements to existing products;

4) Process R&D, i.e. R&D to lower the cost of your manufacturing or operations;

5) Customer R&D, i.e. work your scientists and engineers do with the customer to tailor products to the customer's needs and applications.

This framework goes a long way towards making them "speak English" and think about their projects in business, profit-oriented terms. By the way, a hint: The best, most profitable companies spend a lot more than their competitors on Category 5 (Customer R&D), and Category 4 (Process R&D), and a lot less on Category 1 (Basic R&D). They usually spend somewhat more than the competition on Category 3. Mediocre or worse companies usually reverse this pattern.

Here are a few other ways for you to figure out whether your R&D or engineering organization is profit-oriented:

- Who gets rewarded (promoted, pictured in the internal R&D newsletter, etc.) in the R&D organization: The engineer who makes a scientific (but not commercializable) breakthrough, or the one who refines your manufacturing process to reduce cost half a cent per pound of product? Usually it's the former. It should be the latter.

- How well does your R&D or engineering organization transfer technology (i.e. *learning*) from one part of the company to another? As a general rule, technology transfer is not a priority to scientists: They all like to invent things *themselves*. Put in place a good system for sharing technological improvements in Business A with Business B, or in your plant in Alabama with your plant in Barcelona, and you'll probably find you only need half as many scientists.

- What is your "technology mission statement": To advance technology, or to make
  money for the company in specific, cus-
  tomer-oriented and cost-saving ways? All
  the communications and all the leadership
  of the technology organization — starting
  with you — should be focused on the latter,
  more tangible goals. The scientists or engineers won't do it by themselves, because
  it's not in their nature or training. Unless
  you take a personal interest in maximizing
  the bang for the buck from your R&D dollar, you're wasting an awful lot of money.

By the way, unlike some other areas, you'll meet
relatively little resistance in R&D. Scientists as a
rule are very bright, very well-intentioned people.
Every time I've worked with an R&D organization to
explain the company's mission and their role within
it, they've gotten the point almost immediately, and
have worked constructively to make the necessary
changes. Scientists are often relatively apolitical:
All they need is your good leadership.

STEP 32

EVERYDAY EXPENSE ITEMS

There are a myriad of "everyday" expense items which together represent large profit potential (i.e. savings). Also, by cutting these everyday items, you signal to the organization the seriousness and the philosophy of your overall cost-cutting effort. Among others, I recommend the following steps:

- *First-Class Travel.* Outlaw all first-class travel for everyone, including yourself. I travelled first-class for ten years, and enjoyed it. I switched everyone, including myself, to coach, and got used to it in a matter of months. You can work just as productively in coach if you put your mind to it, and can also buy — for a few bucks — as many drinks as you want. More often than not, you can get a couple of seats to spread out over, particularly if you're polite to the airport check-in person, and you're not reluctant to ask for what you want. When I sit in coach now, it *feels* right: It's consistent with my overall management style. I don't need a wide seat and too much food to convince myself how important I am; a superbly-run company is a much better tonic.

- *Other Travel.* Make sure people really need to go where they're going. Most people like a trip out of town now and then. Make sure it's really necessary.

- *Expense Sheets.* Someone, preferably you, needs to review expense sheets every month. Or spot-check them, and call it a review. When you catch someone billing something inappropriate or excessive, send them a memo: You've been caught, you're forgiven, but you won't be if it *ever* happens again. That employee's expense sheet won't be a problem again for another year or two, minimum.

· *Furniture.* Freeze (i.e. *stop*) all company expenditures on furniture. In today's times, there is always another unoccupied office from which you can take a desk or table or bookshelf. Given a blank check, people always buy new. Asked to be creative, they always find good unused furniture somewhere in the company. If there is a true need for someone to buy something new, the request will inevitably make its way to you anyway, freeze or no freeze. Put in the freeze, and let worthy exceptions bubble to the top; *not* the other way around.

- *Office Supplies.* I've talked about this earlier. I have *never* seen a company that cannot comfortably withstand an immediate 40% reduction in its office supply budget. Just do it. People will adjust rapidly. (By the way, at some companies, the *office supplier* comes in and takes inventory and writes his or her own order. *Never* let a supplier do that, for obvious reasons — Is the supplier's incentive to write as small, or as large, an order as possible?)

- *Copiers and Office Equipment.* Do you really need as many copiers or as much other office equipment as you have? Can't people walk a little further to make their copy? (Better yet, maybe the longer walk will cause them to make fewer copies.) Cancel or don't renew some of those copier contracts.

• *Maintenance Contracts.* Cancel or don't renew all your maintenance contracts on copiers, personal computers, and office equipment. How do you think the price for those contracts is calculated? The suppliers actuarially determine the parts and labor likely to be needed over the life of the maintenance contract, then add in a considerable premium for the "insurance" you are buying (i.e. you are paying a premium to eliminate the risk of being higher or lower than the actuarial average). However, copier (or whatever) repair is a relatively low ticket item, and you don't need to insure against that risk. There are much *greater* risks and dollars in your business which you don't insure against. As a general rule, insure only *big*, potentially devastating risks. Self-insure everything else, and put the saved premiums in the bank.

- *Subscriptions.* This has become a cliche, but it's a good one. Do you really need all those *Wall Street Journals?* Can't people share? Does your library really need all those magazines, all those data services, all those reports? At the average company, approximately 75% of subscriptions can be cancelled at no real detriment to the company.

- *Telephones.* First, make sure you are using the low-cost long-distance carrier for your mix of phone traffic. Second, downgrade your phone *equipment*: Does everyone really need phones with all those buttons and capabilities? Most people don't use them. Finally, publicize a policy outlawing long-distance personal calls. Then spot check phone bills, and when you catch someone in violation, issue a stern memo saying that the next violation will result in a serious penalty. Do that with 2% of your employees and word will spread very quickly to the other 98%. At one company I've worked with, the long-distance bill went down *50%* the first month after such memos were issued.

- *"Contracts" With Suppliers.* Never sign one unless you have to, and discourage your employees from signing them as well. Conditions change, and good business people (purchasers and suppliers) are flexible. A contract locks in a cost you may not need later on. Contracts also make it harder for you to correct mistakes. If one of my employees makes a cost mistake (spends money on something we didn't need), I can stop that spending. If he or she has signed a two-year contract, I'm stuck with that person's mistake for a long time.

STEP 33

OFFICE SPACE

In the U.S., we have a crazy notion about the office space each of us needs. People who travel three or more days a week have their own (unoccupied) office. (In fact, very few people in your organization truly need their own office.) Offices are larger than they need to be. Reception space is often wasteful and unnecessary.

The office space rules which you should follow are straightforward. Choose a lower-cost suburban location. Double or triple people up whenever possible. Eliminate unused "airy" central space. Office size should be functional, not luxurious. Productivity will go *up*, because people sense a more serious and less wasteful work atmosphere.

Finally, think twice or three times before having your business invest in its own office real estate. In most areas, renting is a buyer's market. Your needs change, and you don't want to be stuck with too much or the wrong space. Owning your own building is a nice ego trip, but nine times in ten it comes back to haunt you financially. There's an old adage that says if you're not in the real estate business, don't pretend that you are.

STEP 34

DO YOU WANT TO CATCH PEOPLE'S ATTENTION? GIVE UP YOUR OWN OFFICE

I used to have my company's largest office: Lots of space, unique carpeting, expensive furniture. Years ago, as part of a cost-cutting initiative, I gave up the office. In fact, I gave up *any* office! I'm the head of the company both in title and in terms of day-to-day operations, but I don't have an office.

My secretary keeps all my files at her desk. When I'm in the office and not traveling to a client, I use the office of someone who is traveling. If I need to have a meeting, I may borrow a conference room. It works perfectly fine, in many ways better than being isolated in my former cavernous enclave.

Do you have any idea how much credibility this gives me when I say no to someone's cost request? It shows them *I'm* serious about cost reduction, and I'm willing to take my own medicine.

If you're bold and serious about making money, try this. Nothing will make it clearer to your employees and to yourself that you are serious about maximizing profits.

STEP 35

"SIGN" ALL THE CHECKS YOURSELF

The first several times that I cut costs in my own company, I used all the techniques described above. The most recent time, I added one more wrinkle: I started "signing" all the checks myself.

I don't mean that I *literally* sign all the checks. My payables person signs the checks. However, she literally brings *every* bill, and *every* check to be signed to me for my approval before she's allowed to sign it. We meet twice a month for half an hour, and get through all of them (*very* efficiently) in that time.

This added wrinkle has made a big difference. In

the past, when I was looking at cost reports but not the bills and checks themselves, a lot of things got lost in the category aggregations of those cost reports. When you look at each bill, you'd be amazed at the number of unnecessary "hidden" expenditures that you find. It also gives you a much better sense for real money flowing out the door, and suddenly things that it felt like you *had* to have begin to seem expendable.

If your business is too big to sign all the checks, then "sign" half, or a quarter, or 10% or 2% of the checks each month. But do it. You'll find a lot of savings, a lot of profit potential, which you didn't know was there.

STEP 36

CAPITAL EXPENDITURES

The accountants of this world have done no greater disservice to the successful management of corporations than by creating a category of costs called "capital expenditures." A manager who spends one million dollars on an expense item sees profits go down, right away. A manager who spends a *billion* dollars on capital loses nothing, according to the accountants, until the depreciation starts to kick in.

Capital — plant, property, and equipment — costs real money. It needs to be managed as vigilantly (actually *more* vigilantly, as the numbers are usually much larger) as any expense item.

Yet large companies are often remarkably blasé about controlling capital spending. I once designed a system to evaluate proposed capital spending for an eight billion dollar company. The CEO said to me afterward, "You know this is the first time we really asked ourselves whether each capital proposal *really* is needed, whether the money really needs to be spent." That's a remarkable statement, given the billions of dollars this company spends on capital.

Another senior executive at the same company (a Group Vice President) prides himself on being a very tough controller of costs, and he is. *Except* when it comes to capital. There, he asks for (and gets) four hundred million dollars every year, without any solid justification of the likely return on that capital. He puts his people through pure hell when they ask for another fifty thousand dollars for market research or another million dollars for advertising. But he spends *four hundred million* dollars on capital with only a fraction of the same scrutiny.

Capital is real money. The numbers are big. Scrutinize your capital budget intensely, and you'll add millions of dollars to your true bottom line.

STEP 37

ACCOUNTS PAYABLE

One easy way to lower your costs this year (although it only works once) is to extend your payables. Most suppliers will wait a long time for their money rather than lose you as a customer.

Keep extending your payables: to forty-five days, then sixty, then three or six months for those suppliers who will tolerate it. Never pay a bill until the supplier asks for it at least twice. You'll be surprised: A few suppliers will take as much as *two years* before they finally get around to asking for their money.

STEP 38

DEPLETE INVENTORY

Here's another one-time boost for the bottom line that can help you a lot, *this year.* Make sure before you order an item that you've got your inventory of it running as low as it possibly can. This applies everywhere, from your factory to your office supplies.

The people who place orders in your company don't think this way. They order "just to be safe." They order large quantities, merely so they don't have to call the supplier again any time soon.

If you extend your payables thirty days and reduce your inventory fifteen days, then you've just

reduced *this year's* costs for goods and services by
$(30 + 15) \div 365 = 12\%$.   If your accounting system
doesn't report cost and profit that way, then ignore
it, because your accounting system is wrong. You're
effectively "not buying anything" for forty-five days,
and that's forty-five days of costs which you've
saved, *permanently*; and that savings truly goes
right to the bottom line.

STEP 39

IF YOU NEVER FIRE AN EMPLOYEE, YOU CAN'T HAVE AN EXCELLENT BUSINESS

It's time to turn to people, a potentially more painful and less inanimate source of cost savings.

Way back at the beginning of this book, I discussed the need for a "meritocracy" (rewarding people differentially, based on performance) in order to produce an excellent organization and excellent results. In any organization with more than a few people, there inevitably are employees who are not up to snuff, *particularly* if your standards are high, as they should be. It is impossible to credibly communicate to your employees that you believe in a meritocracy if those non-performing employees get to keep their jobs and salaries.

If you hire right, train well, and know how to motivate, the number of times you'll need to fire someone will be few and far between. My standards are as high or higher than anyone's, and in fifteen years I've only had to fire 3% of all the employees my company has ever had. *Zero* percent, however, is the wrong number — it will lead to dysfunctional behavior in your organization.

I've fired very few people, but each was justified, and the positive "ripple" effect of that firing on the rest of the organization was profound. Each time it's happened, one can almost *tangibly* feel everyone else step up their performance another couple of notches. Those close to the "bottom" do so because of fear of losing their jobs. Those near the top — secure in their jobs — do so because they are heartened that poor performance does not go unpunished. It invigorates them to do well for the sake of the company, a company which truly *is* a meritocracy.

Years ago I had two high-level managers in one area of my company. One of them, whom I'll call Al, had a lot of innate talent, did a decent job, but somehow couldn't get motivated to realize his true full potential. I tried every way I knew to motivate him, and none worked. A second manager, Michael, was not performing. He made a lot of noise and "did a lot of things," but he wasn't truly contributing to the bottom line.

I fired Michael. (To ease my conscience, I gave him an overly generous, outstanding severance package.) The next week, Al was in my office asking, "Am I going to be fired, too?" I sat down and listed the five things he needed to accomplish to avoid being fired. He accomplished all five in three months, and today is an outstanding performer and valuable member of the company, to his and my mutual benefit.

Al *always* had the innate talent. However, as long as he believed he could coast and be treated about the same as everyone else, he coasted. When I showed him that we were a true meritocracy —

that strong performance was rewarded but that poor performance resulted in being fired — his own mental blocks finally dissipated, he became and stayed motivated, and his true innate talent shone through.

If you *never* fire an employee, you will not achieve excellence for your business (and will *certainly* not maximize profits).

STEP 40

KEEP HUMAN RESOURCES SCARCE

There are two types of things an employee can do with his or her time. The first thing an employee usually does is fill his or her schedule with useful, productive things which truly help the company's bottom line. If not enough of these can be found to fill the day, the employee finds lots of other things to keep and appear busy, and now the day is filled.

The same is true from a management perspective. Given a group of employees to manage, the manager first makes sure that all the truly important things get done, efficiently. But wait — there are still more people I can use! Either I'll have some unimportant things get done or I'll do the important things *inefficiently* by throwing more people at the task than I truly need.

I solve the problem this way. When part of my (or a client's) organization asks for another person, I say no. When they ask again, I say no. When they ask a third time, I say no a third time. When they're virtually *screaming* that the added resources are needed and they can't function to the right level without them, I investigate, and often (but not always) let them hire more people.

What this does is drive *inefficiency* and *unneeded work* out of the system. A truly busy employee is forced to prioritize, and do only the truly worthwhile things. More importantly, a manager with scarce resources reporting to him or her is forced to prioritize and to get things done efficiently. In other words, that manager is forced to manage well.

Excessive, unchecked, or non-tightly-controlled staffing leads inevitably to lazy management and inefficiency. Parkinson, who coined the phrase, "Work expands to fill the time available," also came up with a second law: "Work expands to occupy all the *people* available."

When's the last time someone ever came to you and *volunteered* that he or she had more people than they needed in his or her department? The *only* way to promote efficiency and eliminate unnecessary work and motion is to keep human resources scarce.

STEP 41

SETTING SALARIES

In a truly well-run business, setting salaries requires a balance: a *generous* balance. You cannot credibly call yourself a superb business, ask everyone to focus on profits and give up wasteful conveniences and unnecessary perks, and then say, "Oh, by the way, this also means we're not going to pay you very well." You have to pay generously, so that people feel that they share in the benefit of creating a highly profitable business.

However, a balance is also required. If generosity becomes automatic and across-the-board, if pay becomes disconnected from performance, the whole culture, the whole system, and ultimately the bottom line will come tumbling down.

Setting salaries in superbly-run businesses requires three rules:

1) For *groups or levels of employees who have a direct impact on your company's bottom-line performance*, average pay should be *far more generous* than for similar positions in other companies. These are the employees whose presence and enthusiasm you must retain at all costs.

2) For *other groups of employees*, you should be *more generous than most other companies*, but don't need to be "off the map."

3) *Within* any level or group of employees there must be *wide disparities in salary*, tied to demonstrable differences in performance and contribution to the bottom line.

By the way, being very generous — with either group of employees — doesn't mean being fickle or a pushover in negotiating their salaries. Set the levels high, and give people what they deserve. If someone truly critical demands more, give in only rarely and only if you truly believe the increase is justified. Critical is one thing, but *irreplaceable* is another. As someone very wise once said, the graveyards are full of irreplaceable people.

Now many of the pieces of your company culture are beginning to fall in place: We believe in profits and efficiency, and not waste. We believe in hard work, but not long hours. We believe in a meritocracy — you'll be rewarded if you deserve it, but not if you don't. And we'll get rid of unnecessary perks (you'll get used to flying coach and using a former employee's furniture), but we'll pay you *very* well.

Above average people will *love* working in this culture, and those are *precisely* the people you want to attract and retain.

STEP 42

BENEFITS

First of all, many employees discount the value of many benefits, and prefer hard cash. Pay good salaries, and keep benefits to those few that employees truly value.

Once given, benefits don't need to be treated as cast in stone, never to be re-adjusted. One executive I know deals with inflation in the cost of health insurance the following way: His company has a good health plan, which the company pays for in its entirety. Each year, he announces to his employees, he'll contribute more to the cost of the health plan, equal to the rise in the Consumer Price Index (or general inflation rate) for that year. If general inflation is 4%, he'll pay 4% more for health insurance coverage for his employees.

However, in recent years his health insurance company's price increase has equaled 15% per year. Instead of paying the 15% increase each year, he only agrees to pay 4% more, and tells the insurance company to reduce its coverage (e.g. raise the deductible) so that the total cost comes to only 4% more. That is then the health coverage which he gives his employees for the upcoming year.

Some employees ask him how he can do this, how can he lower their coverage? He replies that he *raised*, not lowered, what he pays for their coverage, by 4%. They argue that, even if he's paying more, their coverage is now less. His reply is, "Well, write your Congressman." His point is that he didn't create the national health care inflation problem, and it is not his problem (at least under the law at the time of publication of this book).

I'm not suggesting that his approach is right for you: Maybe it is, and maybe it isn't. The important lesson is that benefits are not a God-given right and they are not forever fixed. They're one more thing that any intelligent manager has to assess and reassess on an ongoing basis.

STEP 43

NEVER GIVE "REGULAR" BONUSES

There is no less effective expenditure in a company than "the Christmas bonus." At every company where I've seen it implemented, it becomes *automatic* (everyone gets it), *non-meritorious* (who wants to be a tough judge of people at *Christmas* time? Doesn't *everyone* have to buy presents for family?), and totally *expected* and therefore *discounted* by employees. Once any bonus, any reward becomes "automatic," it ceases to serve any motivational purpose, and becomes a tool of bad, not good, management.

I also don't believe in regular quarterly or annual bonuses, even when tied to performance. Once bonuses are regularly set on the calendar, managers lose their discretion and their courage to award the bonuses truly differentially and based on merit.

I am a *strong* believer in bonuses. I manage with carrot *and* stick. However, bonuses are most effective when they are *irregular* and *ad hoc*. Give a bonus whenever it's deserved, and never when it isn't. It will look "irregular" on the calendar, but very *regular* in the motivational sense — bonuses will be received when performance or behavior has merited it. Your employees will appreciate the clear relationship between performance and reward.

Some managers avoid this approach because it requires constant judgment: Who deserves a bonus? Who doesn't? How much? An automatic Christmas bonus is *so* much easier.

Well, any manager who doesn't like making judgments is in the wrong game. I'd rather make qualitative judgments as to who deserves what, based on *performance*, and be right (i.e. fair) 90% of the time, than have an "automatic" but non-judgmental, less-meritorious system that is not subject to question. Better to be approximately right than exactly wrong.

STEP 44

TITLES ARE CHEAP

One of my first mentors told me, "If you don't want to give someone a raise, give them a fancier title. It's often at least as appreciated, and a heck of a lot cheaper."

Titles are cheap. Distribute them generously.

STEP 45

REVIEW — MOTIVATING EMPLOYEES

Let's put it all together. You motivate employees by:

- Driving your business to be the best, and highly profitable;

- Clearly communicating what performance and behaviors are desired;

- Rewarding in a way that is consistent with that communication;

- Rewarding highly differentially across employees, based on differences in performance;

- Paying very well, when it's deserved;

- Furthermore (and I've not talked about this enough), working hard to train your employees, both explicitly and by exposing them by example to the management and life lessons you have to offer.

The message is "Stick with me and you'll learn a lot and be paid generously. What I ask in return is that you strive to be the best, and to help the business achieve its objectives."

These types of words and phrases are fairly commonplace. Managers and business cultures that actually *act* this way are very rare, and they inevitably are the most successful and profitable.

STEP 46

EMERGENCY OR REMEDIAL HEADCOUNT REDUCTION

For a profitable business to keep its edge, an occasional firing is sufficient. For an unprofitable or weakly profitable business to become very profitable, more may be needed. Many managers, even good ones, shy away from massive lay-offs; others don't. You have to decide what you're ready and willing to do, but I have just one observation to offer.

Almost all white collar organizations can eliminate one person in four without any reduction in worthwhile output. Many can handle eliminating one in three or one in two. The reason is two-fold: First of all, much of the work done is unnecessary, while necessary work is often done inefficiently. Second, in almost any organization, the poorest-performing 25% of employees simply aren't very good, and aren't adding much value. (This is of course at least as true of the public sector. I live near Washington, D.C. and can tell you that a walk through any government agency or department would sicken *any* taxpayer's stomach when you see what these people *do* with your money. But that's another book.)

In my heart I believe that I could eliminate one-third of the white collar employees at any *Fortune 500* company, and the result would be huge savings and no diminution of value for the customer or the bottom-line. However, I know many of you will view this as extreme. If you share my view or want this done, please call. If this is too radical for you, forget about it and read on.

STEP 47

ELIMINATE MOST OF YOUR "ADMINISTRATORS" AND "MANAGERS"

There are two types of people in any organization: People who do the productive work, and managers or administrators. The goal of the profit-maximizing manager is to eliminate as many of the latter category as possible.

I recently had a friend tell me that he was thinking of asking me for a job, but had decided not to. In looking at my company's organization, he had concluded that I had salespeople, client account managers, and "workers," but no real managers who *just* managed things. What he wanted to be was a manager.

He could not have paid my organization a higher compliment.

The best and most profitable businesses always have broader management responsibilities and broader "spans of control" (direct reports per manager). They instinctively understand that optimizing efficiency means minimizing the cost of managers who don't directly contribute to customer satisfaction or the bottom line. The best companies have one or two or three superb, instinctively profit-maximizing managers in each business, with very broad, loosely-defined, entrepreneurial responsibilities, and then *very* little hierarchy or bureaucracy. I'll take one good profit-maximizing manager over ten paper-shuffling administrators every time.

Here's one rule a client taught me to help you do away with managers: Every manager should be one of his or her own direct reports. If he's Group Vice President of your European Division, then he should also be Country Manager of (for example) France. If she's COO with a number of functional VP's (sales, manufacturing, engineering, etc.) reporting to her, then she should also be one of the functional heads.

To say it another way, instead of "hiring" or promoting a Group Vice President for Europe, simply make your best Country Manager the Group VP as well. Either way you say it, the point is the same: Eliminate "professional managers" as much as possible. A couple of good ones will suffice. Everyone else should be a "doer" who also manages a little on the side. *In addition to* cost savings, the benefit will be a real-world dynamism in your organization, as people report to managers who "know what it's like out there" and are in touch with the market, and not managers who are familiar only with the ossified "management processes" of the organization.

STEP 48

BE MOST RUTHLESS WITH YOUR INTERNAL STAFF FUNCTIONS

With the exception of money lost through weak price negotiation with suppliers (see above), there is no greater source of lost profit in the *Fortune 500* than in corporate, group, and business-level staffs. At the overwhelming majority of the *Fortune 500*, there are far more people than needed in the legal, human resources, accounting, finance, MIS, and, as previously discussed, technical organizations such as R&D and engineering.

There isn't a large company in America (or the world) that couldn't very profitably survive a dra-

matic cut (say, 25-50%) in the size of these departments. If you are *sincerely* looking to double your
profits, start cutting these departments, perhaps only
5% at a time if you want to be cautious. It will take
the department only two months at most to read-
just its work priorities so that the important work
still gets done, but some of the non-contributing work
is eliminated. You should help this along by making
it clear which work is valued and which work is not.

This over-investment in staff is also true, propor-
tionally, for many small companies. At a small company with a 10% profit margin and 12% of costs
represented by various types of administrative staff,
a 25% reduction in administration (3% of total costs)
equals a 30% increase in profits. Entrepreneurs are
often so focused (and rightfully so) on customers
that they fail to see the huge profit opportunity in
their own backyard.

STEP 49

CLOSE THE "OUTSIDE CONTRACTOR" LOOPHOLE

When most large companies reduce headcount, there is a sudden dramatic increase in the use of consultants, temporaries, and "outside contractors." These often are the same employees you just eliminated, now hired back at three times what you were paying them before.

Any good organization should have *strict* controls on the hiring of these outsiders. There are times when their hiring is justified, but in my experience at *least* 50% of all such hirings are unnecessary and a waste of money.

You must communicate to each part of your organization that when you say they will have sixteen people, you mean sixteen people, not sixteen people plus two temps, three consultants, and two part-time outside contractors. If they *must* retain someone from the outside, then it should only be in rare and well-justified circumstances, and only when approved personally by *you.*

Here's one test of whether hiring a consultant is justified or not: Is what the consultant is doing truly contributing to the business' bottom line, or is he or she merely a confidant and political ally of one person in the business, and serving that person's rather than the *business'* aims? Too often it's the latter; you should only allow the hiring of consultants when it's the former.

STEP 50

CHANGE THE DAY-TO-DAY HABITS OF YOUR ORGANIZATION

There are a number of other "qualitative" things you should do to change the day-to-day habits of your organization, as will be discussed in this and succeeding "steps." Each of them will cut costs, and also will help build an action-oriented, bottom-line-focused culture that deplores bureaucracy and protocol.

For one, discourage typing. Yes, I mean discourage typing. Whenever possible, memos or notes should be handwritten. Who says a manager on the third floor can only communicate with a manager

153

on the fifth floor if his secretary types his thoughts for him? Handwriting your memos will result in *shorter*, more to-the-point memos (a plus) and a savings in secretaries (and office equipment and supplies). Three years ago we outlawed the typing of virtually all memos at my company. At the time, people argued to me that it won't save any money, since "The secretaries are sitting there anyway, they may as well type." Well, three years later we have half as many secretaries as we used to. We gradually weeded out and consolidated as the unnecessary secretarial work was eliminated.

The additional benefit of eliminating typing is that you convey to your organization that we are a no-nonsense, no-time-for-protocol operation: I'm in a rush, I have customers to see and money to make, and no time to waste getting this typed. That's a very positive and contagious message.

STEP 51

STOP THE PAPER FLOW

Seventy-five percent of the internal reports, cost accounting, number-crunching, and "cc's" that are distributed in any business are unnecessary, and a waste of time and money. I have yet to find any company that is an exception to this rule.

Think about all the numbers your cost accounting department crunches. (Actually, you can't, because most of them you and other decision-makers never see. Which makes me ask: If the decision-makers aren't seeing them, who are they being crunched for?) How many of those numbers really influence any decision you'll make this week, month, or year? Very, very few. Yes, you need some number-crunching to meet the requirements of the IRS and, if your company is publicly-held, the SEC. But I have news for you: Cost accountants are crunching many more numbers than the IRS, the SEC, or you will ever need. Get rid of the excess number-crunching — it's a waste of money.

Part of the problem is a misplaced desire for precision. The *vast* majority of business decisions are made, as they should be, based on instinct, judgment, and *rough* numbers. It is a rare decision that requires the precise, detailed stacks and stacks of pages that the cost accountants produce. I believe in what I call an "actionable" level of accuracy: If you're not sure if a number is ten or twelve, ask yourself "Would I do anything differently if I *knew* it was ten or twelve?" If the answer is no, then call it eleven and go on to your next decision.

You must re-organize the priorities of your number-crunchers (and scale back the effort) to focus on what's *really* needed by your real decision-makers.

"Qualitative" data proliferation is at least as much of a problem at most companies. There has been an explosion in Corporate America of mind-numbing reports in strategic-speak and mission-objective-goal speak and human-resources-teaming-alignment-process-speak; reports which, by the way, rarely actually *say* anything. The very first thing I learned when I began working with Corporate America is that people never, ever come out and just say what they mean and mean what they say. Everything has to be couched, positioned, and politicized. Try being direct, blunt, and honest with your organization, and help them learn to respond in kind. Teach them, if they must issue a report or send a memo, to focus on the *content* of what they want to say, and not on the verbal (and verbose) "framework" that their latest consultant has told them to always use. Reports should be direct and blunt, *content*-full and *process*-free.

Finally, don't automatically "cc" (send a copy to) everyone under the sun. I used to be that way. Any time I found an interesting article, a piece of data on a competitor, or wrote a memo, I copied everyone who *might* be interested.

People did the same back to me, and I found myself getting five or ten or twenty such "cc's" a day. Well, no matter how fast your hand can move a document to the trash can, it is a time-consuming, mind-using, mind-*distracting* process to sort through all those "cc's."

Today, I think carefully before I ever "cc" anyone on anything. Is this one of the few things I want him or her focused on, or by sending this to him or her am I watering down my major message and direction? Is it really worth fifteen minutes of his or her time to read this article, or would I rather that time be spent calling another customer? When I *do* send a "cc," it now carries more impact, because people know I must be serious about whatever I'm sending.

Stop the needless paper flow in your organization. Make sure people spend their time on enhancing the bottom line, not on informing and employing each other.

STEP 52

STREAMLINE YOUR MEETINGS

My meeting rules are:

- Make your decisions with as *few* people in the room as possible. Never invite people just to be polite, or out of respect for their "title."

- Keep your meetings very short. Five minutes is often sufficient to make a decision. Thirty minutes almost always is. A three-hour meeting shouldn't be necessary more than once every few months. A superb manager should be able to start and finish thirty "meetings" — if that's what you want to call them — a day.

- *Never* call a meeting to discuss; *only* call a meeting to decide.

In short, stop thinking of meetings as ends in themselves. ("What did you do at work today, honey?"; "Well, I had this long *meeting*, and then left to go to another meeting.") Make decisions, call customers, cut costs, and take actions all day long. If you need to have someone else in the room to do it, fine. When you do, get right to the point, cut off unproductive discussion, and go on to your next "meeting."

STEP 53

STOP "OFF-SITE" MEETINGS

Off-site company boondoggles are rarely necessary. They are costly, take valuable people away
from customer-focused and profit-producing activities, and worst of all, convey a lack of seriousness
and lack of urgency about the business' aims and
purposes.

Those meetings rarely benefit company morale
as much as claimed — many people prefer to be
home with their families rather than on the road.
Morale is important, but there are better and more
accurately-directed ways to build it than the distrac-
tion and waste of an off-site meeting.

STEP 54

THE LAST COST-CUTTING STEP — DO IT ALL OVER AGAIN

The hardest part of all of your cost-cutting initiatives will be the resistance to change you will encounter. People will be afraid of everything you suggest, and will tell you it just can't be done. People will be afraid of even straightforward and *trivial* changes — they're just used to doing business the way they've always done it.

You will, I hope, persist, if perhaps only cautiously. You'll take many of the steps I've outlined above, although perhaps in only *small* steps. You'll be afraid to take other steps.

Then, you'll see an interesting thing happen. After a few months, people will adjust their expectations. They'll get used to the changes. They'll realize it's perfectly possible to do business under the new set of rules (and a lot *easier* to make money).

That's when it's time for you to go back to the beginning and go through the whole list of steps again, to institute a new round of cost cuts. Expectations will re-settle a second time, and you can go back through a third and *fourth* time without reaching diminishing returns.

Even if you institute *dramatic* cost cuts the first time, as I did at my own company, you must go through a second, third, and fourth time. With each new iteration, you discover that what seemed drastic before now seems routine, the angst level has been reduced, and you discover lo and behold that there are other, even greater cost-cutting profit opportunities to realize. Your self-confidence in your own cost-cutting skill also increases, and you reach out to try bolder and bolder things. Over time, the interval between iterations can get longer and longer, but the work of superb, profit-maximizing managers is never done.

By now, it should be obvious that what I claimed at the beginning of this book is true. Cost-cutting and profit-maximization is not rocket science, but rather determined resolve. If you *really* want to double your profits, if you're *stubborn* about it, it's easy. If you're really not willing to do what it takes, either yourself or by hiring someone to do it for you, then it's impossible.

PART IV

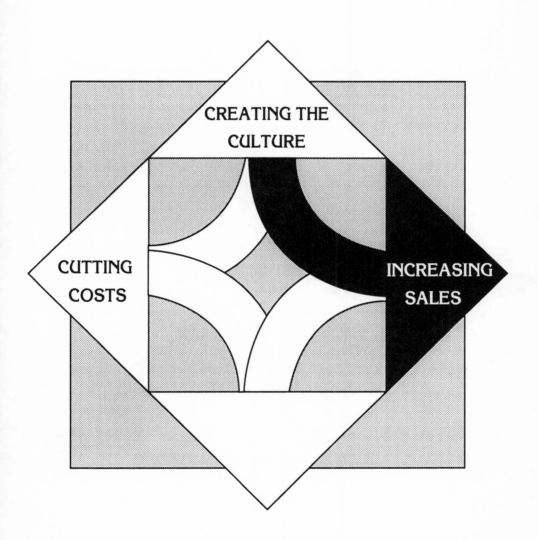

CREATING THE CULTURE

CUTTING COSTS

INCREASING SALES

STEP 55

THERE ARE NO SUCH THINGS AS COMPANIES, ONLY PEOPLE

Let's start with a number of "philosophical" principles which together comprise the mindset you need to maximize the sales of your business.

The first law of superb selling, if you sell to commercial accounts, industrial accounts, distributors, or retailers and not directly to consumers, is that there is no such things as companies, only people. You don't sell your product to some inanimate organization which makes a perfectly rational decision based on the quantitative data. You sell to a human, emotional, somewhat irrational person (or people), who makes the decision in significant part by applying the same issues of ego, personality, and irrationality that he or she does that evening at home when he or she becomes a "consumer."

No single piece of advice has served me better as a salesman than this one. I apply the advice at a couple of different levels, some superficial, some critical.

First of all, when I walk into a prospective client's office, the first thing I do is look at the pictures in the room, usually of spouse and children, and ask the client about those people. There are usually clues in the picture — a school shirt, a tennis racket — that tell you the children's interests and serve as a good starting point for a conversation. I've found that, since I became a father, I've become a much better salesman, because I better understand the joys and anxieties that many of my clients feel as parents, and can form a better bond with them in that initial conversation when I walk into the room.

Other things in the office are invitations to show your empathy with the client: A memento from a sporting event or team, a company award or group company picture, an unusual piece of art. Remember that the mementos you, I, he, or she put in our office are by definition things or symbols of things which occupy a special place in our heart, and which we like to talk about. Because these things are so important to the occupant of that office, you'll find it takes very little effort to get him or her started: The briefest question asked by you will trigger a long story about the daughter, golf game, or whatever else is held near and dear. Just listen well, nod a lot, and show empathy.

And don't forget to flatter whomever or whatever is the object of their affection (and therefore you flatter the client, by implication). Whatever other people might say about flattery, I know one inescapable truth: Flattery works.

More substantively, beyond this initial conversation, always remember that you are selling to a person, not a company. Always get them to tell you the *real* reason they want to buy the product or service you are offering, not the "rational," "on-paper" reason, which is rarely the real reason.

Here's an example of what I mean. A prospective client, the President of a half billion dollar division of a multi-billion dollar company, tells me that he wants me (or one of my competitors) to study ways to make his sales force better. I've done this for clients dozens of times, and I could go away and write him a thorough, soup-to-nuts, *inanimate* proposal on how to study and improve a sales force — which will look more or less the same as the proposals all my (less successful) competitors will send him as well. My chances are no better than one in four or one in five.

Instead, I probe deeper:

"Why do you think you need to make your sales force better?"

"Our market share is slipping, they're missing some good opportunities."

"Why are they missing those opportunities?"

"I know what the sales force needs to do to sell better, we're just not organizing as well as we should to get those things done."

"Why not? What's stopping you?"

"It's, well, we're just not all lined up about this. I know what needs to be done. We're just not operating as a team."

Now I sense I'm getting closer. I go out, a bit, on a limb.

"Who is the obstacle? Joe (the VP of sales, who reports to my client)?"

"*Exactly*. Joe is just *so* old school. The world has changed and he just doesn't see it. And he's sixty, he's going to retire in three years, he's made a lot of money, and he just doesn't give a damn what I think. Nothing I do influences him."

"Why not replace him?"

"I can't. He's snowed George, *my* boss (the corporate CEO). Joe puts on the charm whenever he sees George, and George just doesn't take the time to understand the problem well enough. The charm works, and my better ideas don't sink in with George."

Now the *real* problem has been defined. It's not that my prospective client doesn't know what needs to be done with his sales force, because he does, or he has a reasonably good idea. What he needs is to figure out how to influence, motivate, and manage Joe, and how to better articulate his views and needs to George. In order to do that, we may still do a "study" of the sales force, but I can now write a proposal and do a study that subtly but very effectively accomplishes the *real* aims, not the initially stated ones.

Think about how the prospective client felt when I walked out of his office. What he felt was relief, and excitement: "Finally, here's someone who really *understands me*, who really understands the *real world*, not just someone trying to sell me something." The net result is I *have* sold him something, and he knows that — I haven't *fooled* him. I've sold him something because he sees I'm going to serve his needs more directly and better than anyone else is.

Never leave your prospective customer's office, never stop asking questions, until you get to his or her real, *personal* agenda.

People's *true* agendas come in many shapes and

sizes. Sometimes they are angling for a promotion. Sometimes they are trying to avoid being fired. Sometimes they want something bigger to run, so they are trying to justify an acquisition or investment in a new business area. Often they're trying simply to educate others in the organization as well as themselves so that political infighting can be replaced by teamwork, and they can go home and sleep better at night. All the shapes and sizes, however, inevitably come down to something *personal,* not "rational" or "corporate."

Serving a customer's personal agenda does *not* mean advancing an end you don't believe in. I don't argue for an acquisition that I think is bad for the company just because my client wants it: Rather, I find other options that meet his *and* the company's needs, and convince him that we are more likely to sell these ideas to the company than his less justified idea.

Serving a customer's personal agenda does not mean sacrificing your principles (in the end, that would come back to haunt you). It *does* mean losing your naiveté and realizing that making the sale and truly helping your customer's company don't happen because of sterile, academic, "rational" arguments. They come when you understand the personalities involved. Showing prospective customers that you understand the difference between academia and the real world, that you understand that there are no such thing as companies, only people, is the surest way to build the sales of your own business.

Over the last five years, I've successfully converted 90% of my sales calls into sales. Although there are other reasons, none is as important as my understanding and practice of the principle I've discussed above.

STEP 56

LET HIM KNOW YOU WILL STAND IN FRONT OF
A TRUCK FOR HIM

Think about all the people who have ever worked for you. How many of them can you truly say were *absolutely* dedicated to meeting your needs, who would apply all of their skill and energy single-mindedly to support you? Chances are, the answer is only one or two or a few. And what have you done with those people? Held onto them for dear life, treated them well, made sure they got what they needed.

You need to be one of those people for your customer, or prospective customer.

What I convey to every prospective customer is: If you hire me, you will have the most dedicated, energetic, loyal support person you've ever had. All my skills, all my talents will be directed to doing what you need. I will be even more driven to meet your needs than you are yourself. I'll stand in front of a truck for you if that's what it takes.

Now how many of us can afford to turn away a talented person who is determined to be totally devoted to us? Who would you rather have me working for: you, or your adversary?

Standing in front of a truck doesn't mean giving things away for free. Such skill, energy, and service cost money. However, if you truly convince your customer that you understand his or her personal agenda and you're a talented, energetic, and loyal supporter, you will be surprised at how fast price ceases to be an issue: You'll find your customers fighting battles within their organizations to get *you* more money. Customers will want to make sure they keep you happy, because you're the best thing that ever happened to them and they're scared of losing you.

STEP 57

*BOB FIFER'S FIVE INGREDIENTS
FOR COMPLETING A SALE*

Every time I try to make a sale, I do five things. Do all five, and the sale is yours. Achieve three of the five, and your chances are very good:

1) You must show your *competence*: Your product is good, you're reasonably smart and a nice person, you'll provide good service. This is the most basic requirement: If you can't do this, all else will fail. But competence alone won't get the sale, because many of your competitors are competent, too.

2) You must show you *empathize* with the customer personally. See Step 55.

3) You must convince them you'll *stand in front of a truck* for them. See Step 56.

4) You must make it clear that you don't need them. To say it another way, you *sell by making yourself scarce.*

Five years ago, I got a call from one of the largest companies in the world: a sixty-billion dollar, European-based worldwide conglomerate. The top ninety managers from all over the world were meeting in Florida for a conference headed by the Chairman/CEO. They needed a keynote speaker, I had come highly recommended, and the Chairman had "decided" I would do the keynote address.

Great, I replied, when is it? They gave me a date two months hence, on a Monday morning at 8:30 a.m. (the start of the conference).

Can't do it, I said. I don't travel on weekends, and I can't get to Florida (from Virginia) by 8:30 on

Monday if I leave on Monday morning.

"You don't do *what*?" they asked.

"I don't travel on weekends. That's the time I spend with my family."

The caller went away, told the Chairman this, and called me back. "You don't understand," he said, "The Chairman says there are a dozen outside speakers and consultants who are dying to do this keynote address, and he can choose any one of them. He chose you. This is a great business opportunity. You have to do it."

I replied, politely, "Please tell him that it's good that he has a dozen other people who want to do the keynote address, because he's going to need one of them. Because I don't travel on weekends."

The next call came only half an hour later. "The Chairman says he'll send his personal jet to pick you up and fly you down Monday morning. Will you do it?"

"Sure," I replied.

The plane picked me up at Dulles Airport, the Chairman's limo met me on the tarmac at the Florida airport to take me to the Conference, I gave the speech, and the company became one of my largest clients.

The point of the story is not to avoid weekend travel — that's up to you. The point is that, once they know how good you are, showing them that *you* don't really need *them* is a very powerful aphrodisiac. They think, "If he's that independent, he *must* be really good. But I'll be damned if I'm going to let him win. *I'm* going to win. I'm *going* to hire him, whether he likes it or not."

Here's one other example. I once went on a sales call with a promising but inexperienced younger member of my firm, whom I'll call Ann. At the end of the meeting with the prospective customer, we needed to schedule another meeting. The client said, "How about September 19th?" I looked at my calendar, told him I was booked solid for the next six weeks, but could probably pull some strings and free up part of the 19th for him. And I said it in a reluctant tone, like I was doing him a personal favor. Ann never took out her calendar (she was new in the firm and had almost no commitments booked — her calendar was empty). She merely smiled and said, "Sure, the 19th is fine."

On the plane home, I told Ann to *never* let a client sense that you're not busy. *Always* appear very busy, very much in demand, whether you are or not.

Scarcity creates its own demand. Availability creates its own ambivalence ("Why is she so available? Doesn't anyone *else* want to hire her? Am I a fool for doing so?")

There's a key moment in every sale where the salesperson has to pull back and withdraw. Just when the customer is getting excited about what you're offering, just when he's beginning to feel he's *got* to have you, pull back either bluntly (We're booked solid and not even sure we can handle your account) or subtly (just when he starts to talk about hiring you, start saying, "*If* we were to start to work for you. . ."). He'll get very nervous and start grabbing you, holding on for dear life. At that point, you've won.

5) *Use "guilt" to transform your personal interest in him into his personal obligation to you.*

Almost all the people I've met, in the business world and elsewhere, like to think of themselves as fair and ethical. They don't sleep well if they believe they've wronged somebody. As a salesperson, you need to hold them to that fairness standard: If you're going to go out on a limb for them, the least they can do is give you a fair (monetary) return for your efforts.

That's the real reason, ultimately, for establishing the personal connection and standing in front of a truck for the customer. Because once you've done that, you can turn around, look him or her in the eye and say, "By all fairness, here's how much money your company should pay me. I've been with you every step of the way and more, I've gone the extra mile for you, now it's time for you to go the extra mile for me."

This "guilt," this innate need to be fair that we all feel, is so strong that you'll never actually have to *make* the quoted statement above. Make the personal connection, stand in front of a truck, and you'll find your customer scrambling to be fair to you at your most subtle suggestion or facial expression indicating that, after all the work you've done for him, you feel you're not quite getting a fair shake. I have some customers who ensure that I get a "fairer" shake than I would ever dream of asking for myself.

Think about these five ingredients to completing a sale. Sleep on them. Internalize them. Make them second nature. You'll find yourself with more business than you know what to do with — a nice problem to have.

FIVE INGREDIENTS
TO COMPLETING A SALE

① Show your fundamental competence

② Show that you empathize with the customer *personally*

③ Stand in front of a truck for the customer

④ Make yourself scarce

⑤ Use "guilt" to transform your personal interest in him or her into his or her personal obligation to you

STEP 58

THERE ARE NO SUCH THINGS AS PEOPLE, JUST PEOPLE'S PERCEPTIONS

Even though you may sell your product through a wholesaler or retailer, some products are ultimately purchased by the "consumer." The key law with consumers is that the purchase is always, by definition, irrational, because people (unlike computers) are not entirely (or even mostly) "rational." What matters ultimately is people's perception of what they're buying, not what they're buying itself.

How many of you have Clorox bleach in your homes? For those of you who do, why does your household buy that brand? Chances are you can't answer. The likely *real* reason is because your parents or your in-laws had Clorox, so when you or your spouse started your household, you assumed it must be the right brand to buy.

Clorox sells at a considerable premium over many other chlorine-based bleaches. The true, "rational" advantages of Clorox over those other products are non-existent or relatively negligible: Bleach is bleach. Yet generation after generation buys Clorox because of the cumulative impact of advertising and inertia: If we don't buy Clorox, our whites won't be white, our kids may flunk out of school, and our marriage will likely end in divorce.

To paraphrase H. L. Mencken, "No one ever went broke underestimating the intelligence of the American public."

The power of brand image in consumer products is *huge*. Strong brand images are very hard to achieve. Once you achieve them, they have a powerful inertia all their own. It's *very* hard to *dislodge* a competitor with strong brand image. Hence, brands like Clorox, Crest, Kleenex, Jell-O and McDonald's tend to retain their strength for a long, long time. And brands in relatively new categories like Pampers and Huggies (disposable diapers) spend small fortunes establishing brand image, because they know that once they've achieved it, it will be with them a very long time.

Brand image is a *particularly* strong barrier to competition because of the risks a new entrant faces when it tries to overcome the entrenched competitor's brand image. The reason is that the way you establish brand image is through advertising, and advertising has *no "salvage value."*

If the cost of entry is $100 million to build a new plant or invest in product and inventory, and if a competitor's entry into the market doesn't work, the competitor can earn a fair portion of its money back by disposing of the inventory and finding another use (or buyer) for the plant. If the cost of entry is $100 million in advertising (because the entrenched product's barrier to entry is brand image), and the entry doesn't work, that $100 million is gone forever: There is no salvage value. That is why consumer brand images last so long: It is often too hard and *too risky* to try to overcome them.

I give a lot of seminars, and I once had an attendee who said, "Well, brand image works in consumer businesses, but not when you're selling to companies. Companies are rational purchasers."

Nonsense. The purchasing agent at Company X is the same person who buys Clorox bleach at home. Try telling Federal Express or Xerox that brand image has no value in commercial markets.

In fact, I responded to the seminar attendee this way: Suppose you and I started a copier business, and called it Bill & Bob's copiers. Then suppose we went to the CEO of Xerox and offered him the following deal. We give him five billion dollars, and we henceforth get all rights to use the Xerox name. He has to call his company and copiers "Bill & Bob's" from now on. Would he take the deal?

The attendee thought for a couple of seconds and said, "No, I guess not." So I said, "We now know that the Xerox brand image is worth at *least* five billion dollars," and it's probably worth a lot more.

I had a marketing professor in business school who said, "There's only one thing you ever need to know about marketing. You're selling the customer a $3/8$ inch hole, not a $3/8$ inch drill." Customers don't buy products, they buy the satisfaction of their needs. At one level, their needs are tangible: The hole they need. At a deeper, more fundamental level, their needs are psychic: I want my friends to see me driving an Audi; smoking Marlboro makes me feel like I'm out West with the Marlboro man; taking my kids to a baseball game reminds me of when my Dad took me.

At my company, we have a saying which we repeat all the time: Sell the hole, not the drill. Anyone can make a drill. Only an enlightened, good sales-person can sell a hole well. Sell the hole, and you'll have more customers, and higher prices.

STEP 59

NO TWO CUSTOMERS ARE ALIKE, SO TAILOR YOUR OFFERING AND YOUR SALES PITCH

Most companies are lazy in defining their product or service, and how it's sold to their customer base. They come up with a good idea or two (hopefully), and then try to sell it the same way to everyone.

In many industries, there's enormous opportunity for the company which better meets the needs of individual groups of customers. Tailoring not only the product but also the terms of sale, the level of service, and the way you interact with each customer or group of customers is something many companies don't practice enough.

This is particularly true in service industries, where market research and detailed customer segmentation generally has not reached nearly the level of sophistication achieved at a consumer products company like Procter & Gamble.

The busy businessperson stops at a grocery store on the way home from work. It's Friday evening, the lines are long, and he or she has to wait twenty minutes to pay for the groceries. Why not have a "5% premium" line for people in a rush? They pay $2 extra for a $40 cart of groceries, and they're out in three minutes. The premium more than pays for the cost (it's not even clear there *is* an extra cost, if you think about it), and you've built loyalty in a new segment of the market. The more regular shoppers who can't afford the 5% or are in no rush can wait in the regular lines.

If you think about it, there are dozens of examples like this which you encounter every day of your life. Why don't often-called numbers, where you have to wait ten or fifteen minutes for an operator, have

"900" (toll call) express service for 75¢ where some-one picks up right away?

Does everyone need to receive his or her mail at home *every day*? Why not a small tax rebate for anyone willing to accept every *other* day delivery? (I can guarantee you that if Americans knew the tax and postage savings of cutting mail delivery by 50%, Congress would pass a law and we'd all agree to wait an extra day before receiving our bills in the mail.)

The segmentation of the service sector, the tailoring of services to customers' needs, is a tens-of-billions-of-dollars profit opportunity waiting for some-one who wants to make the money. (Just ask the original investors in Federal Express, who were the first to segment the mail delivery business in the *other* direction.)

The profit opportunity in tailoring extends beyond services. I consulted at a large oil company to the head of its "retailing" business (i.e. gas stations), and was stunned by the lack of consumer sophistication: Engineers were making marketing decisions.

The three-hundredth best marketing person at P&G or Philip Morris could have taught this division a *ton* about how to attract customers and make more money — and could have been hired away at a *very* reasonable price. When Apple hired John Sculley away from Pepsi to be CEO, they demonstrated their understanding that knowing consumers is more important than knowing computers.

Even consumer product companies which have been segmenting and sub-segmenting their markets for decades have lots of uncaptured opportunity. They are only now beginning to think about segmenting the "service" end of their business — how to sell to different channels, what channels they offer their customers to choose from, different ways to pay for products and earn discounts — as well as they think about how to segment the product itself.

Coming up with a good idea, a good product or service, is the first step. *Maximizing* your profit means creatively and energetically tailoring that good idea to every possible (and profitable) segment of the market.

STEP 60

THINK ABOUT HOW YOU SELL

I think of selling as an explicit science, and encourage my employees to do the same. It's not a
science in the sense that it's quantifiable or completely "knowable" with certainty. However, just
because it can't be quantified doesn't mean you
shouldn't study the sales process just as hard and
just as thoughtfully: What makes my customer tick?
What did I do in this sales call that worked? What
didn't? What can I do better next time? Why *do*
people buy the things they buy?

One of the ways I ask and answer these questions is by reflecting on *my* purchases (or non-pur-

chases) from various providers of products and services. Why did I choose that real estate agent or architect? Why did I reject that other one even though he was obviously more qualified "on paper"? What *about* that store display or TV ad caused me to make that impulse purchase? What is it in the way the sales clerk acted that caused me to walk out of that store empty-handed even though I walked in intending to buy something? Every time I ask and answer one of these questions, I learn something about how to sell which I then apply to my own business.

A second way to learn selling is to study the masters: Ronald Reagan, Mikhail Gorbachev, Bill Clinton, and Margaret Thatcher; or Shaquille O'Neal, Greg Norman, Frank Sinatra, and Madonna. These are all people who have achieved a level of success and popularity far greater than other people who can think, play golf, or sing just as well. What is it they're doing or saying that causes a significant chunk of the population to give them its money or votes? Every time I see them, I watch their facial expressions, their mannerisms, the things they say, the way they think, and adopt elements that I think would improve my style. (Well, maybe not Madonna's.)

A key to maximizing sales is to see sales as an explicit, complicated process that offers infinite, never-ending opportunity for you to get even better. The role models are all around you: study them, learn, borrow and steal. Your next 20% increase in sales lies in how well you learn these lessons, not in accidents of fate or in more mundane things.

Every time I *lose* a sale, I force myself to think about why I *really* lost it. At what key moment did I offer or say the wrong thing? Then I resolve never to make that mistake again. Never make mistakes, and you're not stretching yourself very far. Never make the same mistake twice, and you're maximizing your own ability and your business' success.

STEP 61

CUSTOMERS CAN SMELL ONE PART OF BLOOD IN A MILLION PARTS OF WATER

I once heard that a hungry shark can smell one part of blood in a million parts of water, and therefore can find its dinner from far, far away. Customers are the same way. Let me tell you what I mean.

You must convey to customers in every way possible that you are CERTAIN, BEYOND A SHADOW OF A DOUBT that if they buy from your organization they will wind up not only satisfied but THRILLED. You convey this many ways: by your words, your tone of voice, your body language, your written communications. (I have a sentence I include near the end of many of my letters to prospective customers: "I am certain that we will more than meet your needs," and more than a few have commented to me that the word "certain" had an impact on them.)

If you convey *100%* confidence, your customer will be reasonably assured. If you display 99.9% confidence, he or she will be very, very worried. Like a shark smelling blood, the customer can detect the *slightest* doubt you are feeling, and mentally will magnify it a hundred times. Your chance of making the sale just went way, way down.

Many of my clients and prospective clients are out of town, so I take a plane to go see them. As the plane is descending, I take out a pad of paper and pen and write down my "swing thoughts." (A good golfer has a short list of thoughts that he or she focuses on while taking a swing. Unfortunately, swing thoughts have worked for me in selling better than they have in golf.) My swing thoughts never are "Remind them that the product comes in red as well as green," or "Offer to give them terms of 2%

ten, net thirty." The swing thoughts always are something like "Show no doubt," "Be certain we're the best company in the world to meet her needs," and "Forget that you have a sore throat, that you got four hours of sleep last night, and that you have some fire to fight back in the office. Smile, be positive, make him enjoy being around you." When it's all said and done, conveying certainty and ultimate confidence about what you're offering is more important than everything else you say to the customer.

Prospective customers ask a lot of questions. Every answer you give is a potential showing of the "one part of blood." Concentrate, be unwavering, never let the confidence you convey dip at all.

One of the great movies of all time is "Rebel Without a Cause," starring the late James Dean. Dean plays a teenager whose family has moved and who finds himself in a new high school surrounded by a cruel gang of kids. The kids submit him to a series of "hazes" and intimidation, but he's a tough kid and holds his own quite well. They decide to challenge him to a dangerous car race near a cliff, and ask him, "Do you know how to play chickie-run?" Without missing a beat, he calmly and confidently replies, "It's all I ever do." After they walk away Dean turns to his only friend (played by Sal Mineo) and asks, "What's chickie-run?"

When a prospective customer asks you if your company can meet such-and-such a need, the *only* correct response is "It's all we ever do." There's plenty of time to figure out how to meet the need after you leave the customer's office.

STEP 62

THE SELLING PROCESS IS YOUR BEST CHANCE TO SHOW THE CUSTOMER WHAT YOU CAN DO

My competitors frequently take *a couple of weeks* to write a "proposal" (a detailed bid to a customer) for a big project. What does that tell the customer about their efficiency, their ability to react quickly, their ability to be customer-responsive?

I have a rule which I rarely break. Whenever a customer expresses interest, either in person or by phone, I have a written response or proposal out the same day or the next day by overnight express. I have been told scores of times, "I can't believe how quickly you responded. That tells me something about the service I can expect from you down the road."

Whatever your selling process is like, it is crucial that you:

- Respond *very* quickly;

- Respond very professionally;

- Make sure every communication which the customer receives during the selling process is of very high quality;

- Communicate in a variety of ways your flexibility and your willingness to do whatever it takes to meet the customers' needs.

Too many salespeople think the "product" or the inherent, inescapable logic of the proposal will make the sale all by itself. In fact, for most customers in most businesses the real determinants of which supplier is selected are the "intangibles" of what is done and *how* it's done. A customer who hasn't hired you before has only one thing to base that judgement upon: what he or she sees of you in the sales process.

The sales process is your best chance to show the customer what you can do. Treat it that way.

STEP 63

"RE-SELLING" STARTS THE MOMENT
YOU MAKE THE SALE

Needless to say, once you make the sale it is critical that you deliver quality to the customer and deliver on your promises. However, the entrepreneur or salesperson who is unduly anxious about delivering the goods will be an entrepreneur or salesperson of limited success.

The moment you make the first sale, all your thoughts, energies and interactions with your customer should be focused on how you make the next sale or sales to the same customer. This doesn't mean ignoring "delivering the goods." It *does* mean "delivering the goods" in such a way that compels the next sale.

It is a subtle but *crucial* difference. The person who is nervous about meeting the customer's requirements, about delivering on the promise, will be apologetic and overly beseeching to the customer. He will emit that "one part of blood" that the "shark" will smell (see Step 61). He is setting the bar too low: "If I manage to deliver this order without a major customer complaint, I've won." Having won, he now has to hit the road to find a new customer for his next sale.

By contrast, the person who makes sure that the "goods are delivered" but *knows* that one way or another, beyond a shadow of a doubt, he can make that happen, will radiate confidence, competence, and a "can-do" attitude. The customer will feel, "If he isn't worried, why should I be?" The balance between customer and supplier is different in this case: The supplier is seen as someone of superior abilities who the customer can look up to and *count on.*

Then your job becomes translating this confidence

in you into more business. From the moment I make that first sale, I start asking:

- What else does my company have that will benefit this customer?

- In what variety of ways, explicit and implicit, should I expose the customer to these other things he or she should be buying?

- How do I become better acquainted with my customer's organization to render me better able to make these other sales?

If you focus first on delivering the goods, then worry about re-selling *after* the goods have been delivered, it is often too late. At that point, you have less opportunity to interact with, and therefore influence, the customer, and in any case, by then many of the customer's impressions have been solidly formed. The confident salesperson starts the next sale the moment the first sale is complete, and in selling, confidence is a self-fulfilling prophecy.

STEP 64

SELLING IS THE ATTRACTION BUSINESS

One sales organization I know uses the following test in its recruiting process: After a prospective hire passes several rounds of interviews and is considered a serious candidate, an excuse is found to place the candidate on a several hour plane flight sitting next to the hirer.

The decision rule is then very simple: If the hirer finds himself or herself wishing the flight were over a lot sooner, no offer is extended to the candidate.

This process may be extreme, but the principle is solid: Each of us buys things from people we like, are attracted to, or at least are intrigued by in some way. By buying from them, we create an excuse to be around them some more. The psychological need to place ourselves in the "orbit" of attractive people is well known by the professionals.

Obviously, creating "attraction" doesn't mean doing anything which compromises your or the customer's personal integrity or ethics. However, like it or not we are people, and we quickly form likes or dislikes about the people we meet. Part of the successful sales process is to project attractiveness, broadly defined, to the prospective customer.

Attractiveness means charisma, manners, a likeable personality. It means a sense of humor, and a well-proportioned interest in current and world events. It means being a good listener, and someone easy to listen to. And, yes, it means dressing well and appropriately, keeping in shape, and being properly groomed.

All by itself, "attractiveness" won't do it for you. But will it help (or hurt in its absence)? Definitely. Think about how, within the confines of your natural personality, you can maximize your attractiveness to the customer. And think about it when you recruit salespeople for your business.

STEP 65

PEOPLE WHO ASK FOR MORE GET MORE

When I was young (twenty-four) I took a four-day course on how to sell. The main thing I remember from the course is one simple maxim: People who ask for more get more.

The *vast* majority of us have difficulty with this rule. We are to some degree shy, uncertain of our skills, and afraid to ask the customer to give us a lot of his money. We feel unworthy: Who are *we* to ask *him* to see us as someone who can meet all his needs superbly?

Our reluctance and failure to apply this rule is evidenced a dozen times every day in our "ordinary" transactions. How many of you have grumbled about airline meals yet never asked for a second dessert or salad, or whichever part of the dinner you actually liked? They'll give it to you every time. Do you wait for an inattentive check-out clerk to finish a phone call or paperwork, or do you ask them (verbally or by the look on your face) to serve you the customer first, then do the other work (which can wait)?

Have you every tried writing a brief note questioning a bill you received for repairs in your home? I do it regularly, and find that the bill is reduced two-thirds of the time. For almost any hotel you reserve you can negotiate a better rate and/or an upgraded room if you just ask for it charmingly and persistently enough.

These are by and large trivial examples, but the price or quantity of your sale to your customer is not trivial. The simplest sales rule of all is to ask for more: More than you've gotten before, more than the customer's talking about, more than your insecure self thinks you deserve. Done intelligently and carefully, asking for more will work spectacularly for you, because the vast majority of people (and therefore customers) aren't willing to ask for more. They'll give you more rather than try to overcome their own insecurities.

Alternatively, try this: If you want the customer to buy X, then ask him to buy X, Y, and Z. Turning you down on Y and Z will require the customer to muster up all the resistance he or she can: Buying "only" X will seem like a big relief, and a big victory. The rule of thumb in my business is, "Ask for 5 to get 2."

The key to making the mental leap to "asking for more" is to overcome your fear of failure or rejection. The key to overcoming your fear of failure is to redefine the task and therefore redefine what constitutes failure.

I tell my salespeople that if they view each attempted sale as life-and-death, as a victory or defeat, then they should be prepared for a life of depression, because for most people in most businesses there are many more "defeats" than "victories."

Instead, you must broaden the definition of each "battle" to five battles, or ten battles, or a month, or a year.

In my company, we track each salesperson's sales as a twelve-month moving average. In other words, what is the person's average monthly sales over the previous twelve months? That twelve-month period includes probably seventy-five attempted sales, and many successful ones. The time period is sufficiently long to get people to focus on their overall track record, not each sales call. Focused on the overall, they fear each individual "rejection" less, and are emboldened to be aggressive and "ask for more."

Sometimes I say to an up-and-coming salesperson: "Think of each *ten* calls as one call. Did *one* of the last ten calls succeed? If so, then your last unit of salesmanship (ten calls) was a success."

This ability to see successes and failures in "groupings" is a valuable mind game to play on yourself. Earlier in my career, I made a lot of money four times a day and lost a lot of money twice a day, but was so driven by a perfectionist guilt that

I went home at night and thought only about my two failures. Then my business prospered, so I made a lot of money eight times a day and lost a lot of money four times a day. I went home focused on the four failures, and was *twice* as unhappy as before!

Somewhere along the way, I learned to see the bigger picture and to balance the failures against the successes. First of all, this made my evenings and weekends happier. But beyond that, it caused me to worry less about "rejections" and to stretch and "ask for more." The result has been bigger successes as well as fewer failures, because my self-confidence became a self-fulfilling prophecy.

Let's turn next to some more specific lessons about how to make sure you are *pricing* your product or service optimally.

STEP 66

PRICING – YOU'RE LEAVING MONEY ON THE TABLE

Most businesses are instinctively revenue-oriented, selling-oriented, and keep-busy-oriented. They are *not* profit-maximizing (although they may say that they are). A corollary of this is that most businesses, in order to get the sale and keep busy, leave money on the table when it comes to pricing.

The first rule of pricing is the simplest and most common sensical, yet most ignored of all: Make sure you're charging every customer the most that customer is willing to pay.

Here's a simple procedure to apply which will

identify considerable profit opportunity for you. List your largest twenty customers. (If you sell a mass-market consumer product, either do this for the twenty largest retailers or distributors you sell to or, if you wish to do it at the consumer level, the largest customer *segments* you sell to.)

Now, for each customer ask yourself, "If I raised the price 2%, would I *truly* lose the customer?" If the answer is no, then try 5%, 8%, 12%, and 15%. If you answer the questions accurately and honestly, you will find that there are some customers which cannot take a price increase but others which can take 2, 5, 8, 12, or 15%. Unless you're doing this already, this opportunity to increase price is waiting for you, because *there is not a salesforce in the world which, left to its own devices, will price maximize.* They are too intent on booking the sale, and may tell you, "What's 2 or 5 or 8 percent, anyway? It's trivial." The answer is that, for a business with a margin of 10 or 15 or even 25%, price increases of that magnitude have a *huge* impact on profits.

I went through this process with the CEO and VP of Sales of a $2 billion engine manufacturer, and they wound up raising the *average* price across their whole product line 4.7%. We started with the twenty largest customers, but worked our way down and wound up doing the largest sixty-five customers, which together represented 98% of total revenue. Our motto throughout the process was: "The goal is not a *perfectly* happy customer, but a profit-maximized one." I worked with that CEO for three years, and years later at lunch he told me that that motto was the single most important thing he learned from me.

Here's another example. A manager of a small business whom I work with hasn't raised the price of her business' services in five years. When I prod her to raise prices, she responds, "But the customers will be furious. Last time I raised prices (five years ago), it was a disaster."

"What happened five years ago?" I asked.

"It was a disaster — I don't even want to talk about it."

"How many customers actually complained?"

"Tons of them."

"How many?"

"Probably a dozen (out of one hundred and fifty)."

"And how many of those customers did you actually *lose*?"

"Well, none of them. They all took the price increase and stayed with me. But, boy, were they angry."

Because a few customers were "angry," she hasn't raised her prices in five years!

We tend to over-react to customer grumbling. There is enormous profit leverage in raising prices: Take advantage of it.

STEP 67

DETERMINE PRICE, THEN PRODUCT OR SERVICE, NOT THE OTHER WAY AROUND

Most people decide what they're going to sell a customer, then try to sell it for as much as possible. I do the opposite.

The first and most important thing I do is figure out the maximum the customer is willing to pay. Then I scope a product or service appropriate for that level of expenditure. That way, I get the most possible price and revenue from each customer, and maximize my business' overall revenue and profitability.

Those of you who took Economics 101 in college

may remember a term called "the consumer surplus." The idea is that different customers are willing to pay different amounts for your product or service. You don't want to charge the lowest possible price to get all customers, the economic theorists tell us, because then your profitability is nonexistent. You also don't want to charge the highest possible price, because then your margin will be high, but you'll only have one customer (the one willing to pay the highest price). So you select some mid-range price which loses some particularly "cheap" customers and gives other customers the product for *less* than the maximum they would be willing to pay. Those customers' good fortune is called "the consumer surplus" — the difference between the price they pay and the higher price they would be *willing* to pay.

Well, this may be good economics, but it's bad business. (As the saying goes, have you ever met a *rich* economist?)

When I'm through consulting for a company, *that company* captures the consumer surplus, *not* its customers. We figure out the price each customer or group of customers is willing to pay, charge that price, then design a price-appropriate product or service offering for each customer or group.

You may ask, "How do I determine what price the customer is willing to pay?" Read on.

STEP 68

ASK THEM WHAT PRICE THEY WANT TO PAY

For every potential sale I've had, I've asked the customer what he or she wants to pay.

There are many ways to do this. One of the following approaches will work with almost every customer.

One approach is to state ranges and let the customer respond. "I've seen a project like this done for $50,000, $100,000, and $200,000, depending on level of detail. So as not to waste my time or yours, give me some sense of what level fits your budget." Usually the response is in the following form: "We can spend a lot more than fifty, but not quite a hundred." You've now gone a long way to knowing what the customer wants to pay: Maybe $80,000, maybe $95,000. You can refine this further by coming back with a narrower range (eighty to ninety-five), and letting them react, or by first selling an $80,000 product and then trying to get them to trade up by offering additional options totalling $15,000.

A second approach is consistent with the "teaming" mentality which has taken over many supplier-customer relationships among large corporations. In this approach, I simply tell the customer what I'm doing:

"It doesn't make sense for me to 'guess' at a price and then scope a product to that price. If I'm too high, we won't do business together, and we both lose. If I'm too low, you're getting less product than you really want and need. We're on the same side here, and need to work together. The more straightforward approach is for you to tell me how much you want to spend, and then I'll scope to that price. We can make any adjustments as necessary."

There are other variations and combinations of approaches, but they all do the same thing. Get comfortable asking your customer to name the price, and learn to avoid pricing your product or services yourself. Remember the following observations of human behavior:

- Never underestimate the power of a direct question. If you ask someone something directly and in a determined voice, the majority of people will feel compelled to answer, and answer honestly.

- Silence can be an enormously powerful negotiating tool. Remember this negotiating rule: "Once the price is named, whoever speaks next loses the negotiation." When you ask for a price, the customer may hem or haw or be uncertain. Just stay *quiet*. Avoid your temptation to help the customer out of an awkward situation. *Don't say a word.* Your silence demonstrates your confidence and resolve. More important, silence is a void that has to be filled. If you stay quiet, the customer eventually — after ten or twenty or thirty seconds — will get around to naming a price.

STEP 69

TO CAPTURE THE CONSUMER SURPLUS FOR MASS-MARKET PRODUCTS, PRICE DISCRIMINATE

A hotel where I stay regularly charges $129 a night. However, they have executive floors for the business customer, where rooms go for $250 a night. What do you get for the extra $121?: A free newspaper and a cold continental breakfast. Total extra cost to the hotel, including labor: less than $5. What a deal, huh?

Yet the executive floors regularly sell out before the rest of the hotel. Many business travelers don't pay their own bill (their company's shareholders do), so they don't care about price. In their subconscious view, they are getting a newspaper and breakfast for nothing, so it *is* a good deal.

The hotel also has a *third* option. Any aggressive, skilled secretary or travel agent who calls up and demands an executive room for the regular (non-executive) room rate of $129 (reminding them how often she sends visitors to that city), gets it. The hotel manager figures, why not (unless the executive rooms *are* booked solid)? The extra newspaper and breakfast doesn't cost me anything, anyway.

The other day, the concierge who puts out the breakfast left the room and ill-advisedly left her list of guests and room rates on the table. It turns out that those of us on the floor — with the exact same rooms and services — were paying as little as *$89* and as much as *$250*. The sole difference was the willingness of the travel arranger to negotiate a good rate.

This example of "price discrimination" is how all good pricers of mass market products need to think: How do I create relatively small but highly visible differences in the various offerings within my product line so that I can capture the most each group of customers is willing to pay, i.e. capture the consumer surplus?

Examples of this are all around us. Overnight express mail 10:30 a.m. service (costs more) vs. 3:00 p.m. service. Super-premium vs. premium vs. regular unleaded gas (Do you *really* think there's that much of a difference?). "Rush" dry cleaning orders vs. the usual three days (try saying you can only pay regular rate, but *really* need it rush. It works every time.) Macintosh computers, of which there are countless variations and price points: My informal survey of friends and neighbors say many go for the most expensive, but few really understand what the product differences are and think out whether the extra money is worth it. And airlines (the masters of price discrimination), where the same seat has ten different prices depending on how aggressively and cleverly you care to buy it.

Price discrimination is to the mass market what "asking what they want to pay" is to the commercial or industrial market. Either way, the goal is to get each customer to pay the most he or she will pay. The profit leverage is enormous.

STEP 70

THE KEY — GET THE HIGHEST POSSIBLE PRICE BUT DON'T LOSE ANY CUSTOMERS

The truly skilled businessperson gets the highest possible price, but doesn't lose any customers in the process. He or she has an offering for each significant category of customer — all the way from those on a tight budget to those who are willing to pay top dollar.

When negotiating price directly with a customer, this means striking a careful balance in what you say: Try to raise the price as high as you can, but don't issue any ultimatums that force the customer to say "yes" or "no." Instead, selling and pricing questions should always be phrased so that the only two possible answers are "yes" and "yes, but at a lower price please." That way, you don't lose any customers.

One way I achieve this is by saying, "Based on everything we've discussed, I think the price should be between twenty and thirty thousand dollars. I'll do it for twenty if you really want because I want your business, but if *I* were you, I'd pay thirty. The extra value will definitely be worth it." There are several possible customer responses to this, but none of them is a simple "no" — you've kept yourself alive, and you're getting the highest price you possibly can.

STEP 71

BE DIGNIFIED ABOUT PRICING

My company has an office in London, and I've consulted for many years in the U.K. The single most valuable lesson I've learned from the British (as well as from some in the U.S.) is that discussing price is "beneath" the dignified businessperson.

The attitude to take is a reluctant, professional, matter-of-fact one. "Oh, by the way, here are some numbers about what it might cost, but what you and I really care about is the professional delivery of quality goods or services. We don't really want to haggle like a couple of people at a bazaar, do we?"

This reluctant, dignified attitude works very well in combination with the "ask them what they want to pay" approach. Your reluctance provides a good excuse to be "silent" (see Step 68), and the customer will usually open up and be honest about what he or she wants to pay, rather than be the first to set off an "undignified" bazaar-like negotiation. If you take the high road, he or she will follow your lead.

A corollary of the "be dignified" rule is to price as late as possible in the selling process. Don't mention price until the customer does. Your mentioning it first broadcasts your nervousness about the price. Your being quiet about price conveys a confidence about what you are delivering and a matter-of-fact assurance that the customer will pay you fairly for it.

STEP 72

REMEMBER — PRICE HAS NOTHING TO DO WITH COST

The evening before my first class in business school, we were handed a case to read and analyze. A manufacturer of bathroom fixtures had three different products, and had to decide how to price each one. We were given a dozen pages of costing data, and stayed up half the night trying different cost allocation schemes to figure out what the right price was for each of the three products.

The next morning at 8:30, the professor walked in and demanded that a succession of us present our pricing schemes. The various students then got

into a ninety-minute debate about which cost allocation methodology was fairest in calculating "true"
cost in order to set price. The professor listened
silently.

As the end of class approached, the professor
cleared his throat and spoke up. "Every one of you
is wrong. When you set prices, you *never* look at
cost. You price what the market will bear." With
that, he left the room.

No single lesson has served me and my clients
better than that one.

STEP 73

MARKETING IS A STRATEGIC COST —
OUTSPEND YOUR COMPETITION, IN GOOD
TIMES AND BAD

One of the great (and unprofitable) paradoxes of business is that business people are focused primarily on revenue, yet don't spend enough on marketing. As noted earlier, the superb businessperson distinguishes between non-strategic and strategic costs. He or she ruthlessly minimizes non-strategic costs, so as to maximize profits and *so as to free up money to spend on marketing and other strategic costs.* Most truly successful and profitable businesses *outspend* their competition in marketing, either in absolute dollars or as a percentage of sales.

All businesses, sooner or later, have down years. That's usually when they look to cut costs, and often the *first* place they cut is marketing, because it's the "easiest." "Let's cut there," a senior executive once told me, "because it's easier to give less money to our ad agency than it is to lay off our own employees."

Nothing could be more ill-advised. Marketing dollars are strategic, and strategic costs are the long-term lifeblood of the business. *Marketing expenditures must be maintained in good times and bad.* Cut everywhere else, but never cut marketing dollars when times are bad.

STEP 74

DON'T BE AFRAID TO USE A SHOTGUN

Too often, the search for new customers is conducted too narrowly. "Why should I advertise *there*? Nine out of ten readers won't buy." Well, often the one in ten is good enough to justify the marketing expenditure. Good marketing often requires using a shotgun, not a rifle.

Do the math for your business, and figure out how wide a shotgun would pay for itself. My company sends ten thousand pieces of (marketing) mail a month, and 99.9% are thrown away. However, the 0.1% that produce new customers *more than* pays for the other 99.9%.

This, by the way, applies to job searches for you or your children. A relative of mine graduated from business school and wanted a job in the Washington, D.C. area. He wrote to the three or four companies that looked "most interesting."

I told him, "Nonsense! You have to spread the net much wider. You never know what you'll find." We got a list of the two hundred largest businesses in the metropolitan area, and sent off a letter and resume to each. (In the era of word processors, it just doesn't take long or cost much to send two hundred letters.) Fifteen companies responded, eight interviewed him, and four gave him job offers. With those odds, writing to "three or four" wouldn't have worked.

Most, but certainly not all, businesses make this mistake. If you've got something worthwhile to sell, leverage it by looking to sell it to as many geographies, channels, and types of customers as profitably possible. Do the math first, but as the math dictates spread your marketing net wide, and worry only about the customers who buy, not those who don't.

STEP 75

INVEST IN YOUR SALES FORCE — NO
INVESTMENT WILL YIELD A GREATER RETURN

There are two theories as to what sells. One theory is that a product has a market of a certain size, and the product's attributes and customers' needs determine the size of that market.

The second theory is that salespeople sell. Every salesperson has a built-in (and financially motivated) need to sell, and goes out and hits the street, has lunch with prospects, hustles, and generates sales. The more salespeople you hire, the greater your sales, regardless of product or market.

Both theories obviously contain a fair amount of truth, but in my experience the second theory is the more often neglected. Most companies *under*-invest in their salesforce, at the expense of revenue and profit.

What does it mean to invest in your sales force?:

1) Make sure you have *enough* salespeople (see the second theory above).

2) Make sure the salespeople spend their time with the customer, not doing administrative work or other things.

I was once retained by a large computer company to solve its selling problem: Customers weren't buying the company's product in the quantities the company wanted.

I gathered a few pieces of data. My client's salespeople were spending 30% of their time with customers; the competition's salespeople were spending 90%. My client's salespeople visited customers twice a year, asking for more sales. The competitors' salespeople visited customers (on average) twenty-one times a year: twice to ask for sales, and nineteen times to see if the customer needed any help with software, a service problem, or a report they had to write for their boss. Of *course* the customer is going to give the majority of his or her loyalty and sales to the competition!

> 3) Hire enough relatively low-paid clerical people to support the salesforce. This frees the salespeople up to spend time with customers.

The third piece of data in the example above: My client's salespeople have one support person for every three salespeople. The competition has *two* support people for every *one* salesperson. That's why *our* salespeople were too busy to give customers the level of service that was needed.

> 4) Compensate salespeople highly variably, as a function of *profits*, not sales.

A hospital products company I consulted to once switched its commission system from sales-based to gross-margin-based (salespeople now got credit for the gross margin dollars of the products they sold, not the sales dollars). Within *one month*, sales of high-margin products were up 28% and sales of low-margin products were down 26%. As a result, overall profits were up 50%.

5) Hire salespeople who understand how to sell and how to make a profit, not people who "know the product." People who truly know how to sell are the rare and valuable ones; anyone can learn the product line.

6) Invest in sales training, focused on true *selling* and *profit-making* skills, not just product facts.

At too many mediocre companies, sales training consists of "product" people unveiling "this year's product line." Try dedicating much of your sales training to the subtle and powerful nuances of how to sell and how to price-maximize. The feedback you will receive will be: "It was *really* helpful — the best training we've ever received."

Here's one other simple thing to do. Get a top salesperson at three companies you admire (in industries other than your own — it doesn't matter, because selling is selling) to speak to your salesforce about the keys to their success. Your salespeople will eat it up, and the results will show in their performance.

For many businesses, the salesforce is the most important asset, more critical to the business' success than the bricks, mortar, and machinery of your plant. Yet we spend millions to maintain the plant and skimp on supporting the salesforce. This is penny-wise and dollar-foolish.

Remember to distinguish between strategic and non-strategic costs. To double your profits, fully support the former, and minimize the latter.

PART V

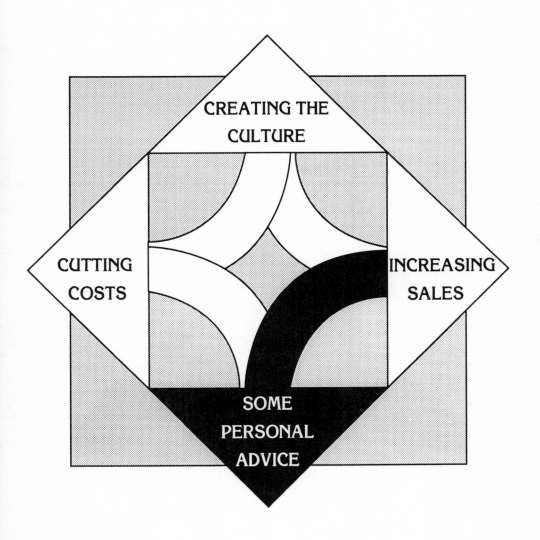

CREATING THE CULTURE

CUTTING COSTS

INCREASING SALES

SOME PERSONAL ADVICE

STEP 76

BE STUBBORN

Since many of the recommendations in this book are challenging to your *mindset* as a manager, I would be remiss to end without a few short pieces of personal advice. What does it take, at a personal level, to achieve the mindset necessary to double your profits?

My first piece of advice is to *be stubborn.*

I once asked one of the most successful businesspeople I ever met what the personal key to his success was. He is brilliant, charismatic, sincere, and intuitive, and I expected him to name one or more of those things.

Instead, he said simply, "I'm stubborn." "You're what?" I asked. "I'm stubborn. I know what I want to achieve. I see a way to get there, and I *believe* in that way. And nothing or no one is going to stop me from getting there, no matter what they do or say."

I asked the same question of another highly successful person, who had succeeded with half a dozen very diverse types of businesses. "People see me as flighty, because I keep shifting my areas of concern and interest," he replied, "but there's one overriding constancy to everything I do. I believe I'm more *determined* than almost everyone else, and *I'm going to find a way to make money off of it.*"

The stubbornness and determination these two spoke of is characteristic of all the successful businesspeople I know. They don't take "no" for an answer, but instead stick to it and wear their uncooperative adversaries down. They have a "can-do" attitude that says there's a way around or over *every* barrier, no matter how daunting. They are so confident in their beliefs that they don't even *enter-*

tain the thought of letting someone else stop them from achieving their goal.

Most people in life and business are ambivalent, struggling to find the principles that they truly believe in. If you can find yours and stick to them stubbornly, you'll be at a natural competitive advantage, and you'll win most encounters regardless of relative skill, experience, or intellect. If profits are important to you, this book offers up one set of principles to believe in.

STEP 77

KEEP WORK IN PERSPECTIVE

Much of what this book recommends requires judgement, subtlety, and the ability to attract other people, none of which usually are optimized by a workaholic. I recommend setting strict limits on when you are willing to work and when you are not, and then sticking to them. More importantly, work must be seen as a distant second (or third, fourth, or fifth) in importance to whatever is truly important to you in life: Your family, your friends, or your favorite recreational activities.

In my experience, the person who has other things in life that are more important: (a) Is in the positive frame of mind necessary to truly do well at work, and (b) Has the proper sense of perspective and detachment necessary to see business as the game that it is, and to play it well. Everything it takes to win in business, and everything this book talks about, requires the trading off of a number of subtle variables: knowing when to apply which rule and which tactic to which situation, and when to offer which carrot or which stick to which employee, customer, or supplier. This isn't math, accounting, or science, where the intellectually-correct, "deterministic" answer is being sought: Rather it's an infinitely variable game of intuition based somewhat loosely on a large set of rules.

The person who lives and dies for work has trouble taking it as a game, because it's his or her life. The balance and trading off that are required are then hard to come by: The player becomes too obvious, too one-dimensional, too crude. The sense of detachment that a more important life outside work gives you allows you the confidence, the calmness, the clarity of thought that makes you a truly winning player.

It may be the world's greatest rationalization (and if so, more power to us!), but I've found that the greater priority you place on things in your life *other* than business, the more money you make. If you get paid by the hour, this isn't true. If you get paid to be a profit-maximizing entrepreneur or manager, it is.

STEP 78

STRETCH YOURSELF, AND HAVE FUN

No one in the world is more depressed than the person who knows he or she has gone as far as he or she is going to go, and can find no more challenges to conquer.

The nice thing about business, and about the subject of this book — maximizing profit — is that the process is variable and subtle enough that it is *impossible* to ever get to the finish line: You can *always* do better.

However, it takes a clever and healthy mind to enjoy a path where you never reach the finish line. It's difficult to conquer the need to feel, "I've completed the job: I got an A in the course."

I derive my enjoyment from always stretching to be better, always trying to re-invent myself to get to the next level. This in turn requires a high degree of introspection, and a *willingness* and a comfort level to be introspective: What am I doing well? What could I do better? What obstacles am I creating to my own success? How do I overcome them? In my experience, managers who are unable to talk about themselves and truly be introspective usually are limited in the success that they achieve. If you can't think about yourself introspectively, how can you stretch and re-invent yourself?; if you can't re-invent, then how can you go to the next level? The ability to be introspective is one of the keys I look for when I recruit.

The set of personal advice in this and the preceding two steps may *appear* contradictory: Be stubborn, but be willing to re-invent yourself. Stretch, but don't take work too seriously.

However, the advice is *not* contradictory. The starting point is to know what you want outside of work (i.e. not take work too seriously), and to know what you want at work (be stubborn). See business as a game, with a healthy sense of detachment. The way to keep the game challenging, to keep it fresh, is to never completely settle in, but to always try to be better: Not because it's life and death, but because that's what makes the game *fun*. Have fun at the game, and you'll be better at it; get better at it, and you'll *more* than double your profits. It works.

Doubling your profits *isn't* a matter of rocket science; it *is* simply a matter of resolve. If you can achieve that resolve and have fun doing it, you've accomplished what relatively few people have. I hope this book has helped start you well on your way to getting there.

I wish you luck. And if you'd like more help, I'd be happy to provide it.

ABOUT THE AUTHOR

Bob Fifer is Chairman and CEO of Kaiser Associates, Inc., a North American management consulting firm, and Kaiser Associates International, Inc., its European counterpart. Both firms specialize in improving the profitability of businesses large and small, through cost-cutting, improved salesmanship and pricing, strategy development, and competitor and customer intelligence. Another affiliate of which Mr. Fifer is CEO, Kaiser Ventures, manages and maximizes the profits of companies and businesses in return for an equity interest in those enterprises.

The philosophy of all parts of Kaiser is simple: We can double the profits of *any* business or company, in six months or less.

Mr. Fifer grew up in New York, where he lived through high school. He received a Bachelor's degree, *magna cum laude*, in economics from Harvard College, and an M.B.A. from Harvard Business School. During the last fifteen years, he has helped more than a hundred of the *Fortune 500* as well as numerous smaller businesses and international corporations improve their bottom line. It is the lessons from these experiences as well as the success of his own companies that formed the basis for this book.

Mr. Fifer can be reached at:

Kaiser Associates, Inc.
1595 Springhill Road, Suite 700
Vienna, VA 22182 USA
Telephone: (703) 827-9400   FAX: (703) 827-9498

Kaiser Associates International, Inc.
36 Upper Brook Street
London W1Y 1PE ENGLAND
Telephone: (44) 71-411 6000   FAX: (44) 71-411 6001

Mr. Fifer welcomes your inquiries and comments.